CONSCIOUS RECOVERY

A Fresh Perspective on Addiction

TJ Woodward

This book may be ordered through booksellers or by contacting

RecoveryBookstore.com
7250 Auburn Blvd #164
Citrus Heights, CA 95610
1-855-REC-BOOK
orders@recoverybookstore.com

Printed in the USA

Revised Edition 6/2019

DEDICATION

With profound respect and gratitude, I dedicate this book
to my friend, mentor, and soul mate, Mary Helen Brownell.
Through her selflessness, she helped me and hundreds of
other people break the cycle of their addictive behavior.
She literally helped change the world, one soul at a time.
Her legacy lives on through my writings and my work.

We use all kinds of ways to escape - all addictions stem from this moment when we meet our edge and we just can't stand it. We feel we have to soften it, pad it with something, and we become addicted to whatever it is that seems to ease the pain.
— *Pema Chödrön,* When Things Fall Apart

CONTENTS

Preface: My Story xvii

Introduction: The Addicted Self 1

What is Conscious Recovery? 1
The Room of Spirit 3
The Outer-Focused Life 5
The Roots of Addiction 7
Cultural Influences 8
Holistic and Integrated Recovery 9
Getting the Most Out of Conscious Recovery 10

Part 1: The Roots of Addiction 13

Chapter 1: Unresolved Trauma 15

What Is Unresolved Trauma? 15
Physical Trauma 17
Mental Trauma 19
Emotional Trauma 20
Spiritual Trauma 21
Vicarious Trauma 22
The Consequences of Unresolved Trauma 23
Trauma and the Unconscious 24
Victim Consciousness 26
Healing from Trauma 27

Chapter 2: Spiritual Disconnection..................................... 29

What is Spiritual Disconnection? 29
Attachment Theory 31
Core False Beliefs..32
Brilliant Strategies..34
Addiction is a Brilliant Strategy 35
Other Brilliant Strategies 36
The Inward Journey 37
Shifting Consciousness...39
A New Way of Being 40

Chapter 3: Toxic Shame 43

What Is Toxic Shame?..43
Guilt vs. Shame.. 44
Working with Shame...46
Sources of Toxic Shame 47
The Impact of Toxic Shame..48
The Importance of Language..49
Pain and Suffering..51
Activating Empathy..52
Bringing Shame into the Light.......................................53

Part 2: Breaking the Cycle of Addiction 55

Chapter 4: Creating Safety 57

Creating External Safety 58
Maintaining an Open Heart..59
Creating Internal Safety 60
Developing Self-Love..61
Overcoming Self-Criticism...62
Embracing Self-Acceptance..63

Rebuilding Trust 64
Engaging in Safe Community..65
Expanding Your Comfort Zone 67

Chapter 5: Unlearning.. 69

Living Beyond Your Stories...70
Evidence or Conclusion? 71
Relative Reality or Ultimate Reality?....................................72
Moving Beyond Limitation 74
Self-Parenting...77
Recognizing the Shadow 80
Stuck in the Shadow 82
Integrating the Shadow 82
Raising Your Conscious Awareness 84
Activating Intentionality 85
Becoming the Observer..88
The Joy of Beingness 89

Chapter 6: Practicing Spiritual Principles........................... 93

What is Nonresistance?...94
Practicing Nonresistance...96
What is Judgment? 98
Practicing Non-Judgment.. 100
Developing Your Own Understanding of Spirit.....................103
What is Mindfulness?..105
Practicing Mindfulness... 106
Practicing Witness Consciousness 108
The Benefits of Presence 109
Living in the Question 110
Practicing the Questioning Process 112
Accepting Impermanence...114
Releasing Control 115

Part 3: A Return to Wholeness 117

Chapter 7: Owning Your Power 119

The Power of Perception 120
Shifting Perception................................... 122
The Power of Forgiveness.............................. 123
Deepening Forgiveness 124
Forgiveness and Accountability 126
The Power of Compassion 127
Feeling Your Feelings 128
The Power of Authenticity............................. 130
Embracing Authentic Wholeness........................131
The Power of Gratitude...............................132
Being Gratitude 134

Chapter 8: The Great Remembering.................... 137

Letting Go 138
Making U-Turns.......................................139
U-Turns in Consciousness.............................141
Embracing Love 143
Nurturing Our Divine Nature 145
Inner and Outer Connection 146
Cultivating Supportive Community.....................148
Perceiving Reality 150
Spiritual Bypassing..................................151
Divine Integration 152

Chapter 9: Awakened Living 155

Finding Purpose 156
Ego and Purpose...................................... 158
Maintaining Focus 159

Conscious Action 161
Choosing Happiness 162
Choosing Peace 163
Discovering True Freedom...165
Embodying the New Paradigm 166
Awakening into Service 168
Engaging an Enlightened Life 170
In Conclusion 171

ACKNOWLEDGMENTS

A special thanks to the spiritual teachers and addiction treatment professionals who have, directly or indirectly, assisted me in the process of writing this book.

I offer deep appreciation for the countless people doing great work in the field of psychology and addiction treatment, especially those who have been personally influential in my work, including Dr. Krista Gilbert, Roland Williams, Dr. Brigitte Lank, and Melissa Stevenson.

Additionally, I want to honor the spiritual teachers and authors who have had a profound impact on my life and on this work, especially John Bradshaw, Brené Brown, Eckhart Tolle, Pema Chödrön, and Byron Katie.

Finally, I am expressing deep gratitude for my friends and family, and heartfelt gratitude to my loving husband, Will Woodward, for his unyielding love and support, and for helping me to open my heart to a new way of being.

Editorial Assistance

Developmental Editor: Dr. Adriana Popescu

PREFACE

MY STORY

I've found that every spiritual advance I've made was preceded by some sort of fall—in fact, it's almost a universal law that a fall of some kind precedes a major shift. An accident, a fire that destroys all the stuff we've worked so hard to accumulate, an illness, a failed relationship, a death or injury that causes deep sorrow, an abandonment, a serious addiction, a business failure, a bankruptcy, or the like. These low points actually provide the energy needed to make a shift in the direction away from an ego-driven life to one full of purpose.

— *Dr. Wayne Dyer,* The Shift

To begin, I am sharing my personal story, which took me from a life of struggle and addiction into a joy-filled, meaningful existence. A movement from loss to recovery, from darkness into light, from a sense of brokenness to reconnecting with my wholeness—from an outer-directed life to an inner-focused way of being and seeing. I start with my story not because it's unique, or even unusual, but because it is not unique. It's possibly a lot like your story. So, I'm starting with my story in the hope that you will find in it things you can relate to and connect with. And from that point of connection, we'll follow the trajectory of our stories through the rest of this book, looking at addiction and its roots and then at how to untangle those roots to rediscover how to live our best lives.

"I've never met a happier child. You laughed all the time." That's what my mother remembers about me. What I remember is lying on the ground in the back yard, looking, for what felt like an eternity, at a butterfly, in awe at its magic. How is all this life possible? What beautiful wings. How much detail must be here for it to fly? How did this come to be? Look at this tiny little body of this ant. Wow, it takes all those ants to build this pile that they call their home. I felt like the luckiest person alive.

I also wondered what the universe was like before life. Before animals, before insects, before plants even—what existed before them? I suppose I was wondering about consciousness before manifestation, the pure consciousness that children have an innate knowledge of. I was probably also asking why the grownups weren't noticing life like I was, why they seemed to be so busy and so angry. But mostly I was filled with curiosity, presence, and awe. Looking back, I believe I was perfectly connected with truth of who and what I was.

Then I started to lose that truth, to begin believing that I wasn't enough, that I was broken in some way.

In first grade, my classmates and I had to change into our tennis shoes before recess. I didn't know how to tie my shoes, and the teacher said, "You need to learn how to tie your shoes by tomorrow." She sent me home with a pair of shoes attached to a piece of wood. I remember, like it was yesterday, feeling "stupid" and "less than" because I had to carry this board home. So, I tried to learn at home. I'm left-handed, and it was difficult, but by the end of that day I thought I had it down. However, when the time came for recess the next day, I couldn't do it. And everyone else could. I felt like everybody knew how to live life but me. This was one of the first times I remember feeling different than everyone else, and somehow less capable.

I remember another poignant experience. This happened when I was seven years old. I sat one evening with my mother and my sisters at the dining room table. As I sat there, I began to shut down. I don't remember what was said or what happened in that moment, but I do remember distinctly the sensation of being overwhelmed with fear, a sense of terrible wrongness, and then a closing down and a walling up. Two distinct thoughts came to me: "This is not safe" and "I have given too much." Looking back, I can surmise that the circumstances of my life had finally overwhelmed my natural joy and resilience. I began to develop beliefs that I was broken or damaged in some way and that the world was not safe. These limiting beliefs were quietly erasing my deeper, instinctual truths. Maybe I was also starting to notice that I wasn't like a lot of the other boys—I was more like many of the girls, and of course I didn't know what to do with that.

So, my experience at the dinner table that evening was the feeling I'd had about the shoelaces, magnified a hundredfold: everyone knows how to "do life" but me. In that moment, I made a decision—to close down, put a barrier around my heart, to disconnect in some way. Of course, this was not a conscious choice, but it happened nonetheless. At that moment, I entered a world of toxic shame, in which I believed myself to be flawed and broken. In the process, I lost my curiosity and my joy—I lost sight of my genuine self.

We come into this world as beings who know and live in acceptance, openness, connection, presence. We are those joyful little children who know in their hearts that they are whole and perfect and that life is wonder-full and wonder-filled. But life has a way of teaching us the opposite; traumatic experiences teach us that we are broken, and this pushes us further from our oneness with Source. Think about what little children are taught about the world, especially children who experience cruelty or who live in a threatening environment. They are taught to be mistrustful, to devalue themselves. They are taught that "might makes right", that strength lies in conquering, in overpowering people and situations. They learn that life is a struggle, it's something to be resisted, and at best it's a challenge—a problem to be figured out and solved. They are taught that there is not enough, and that people need to fight and compete to get what they think they need.

I recently witnessed an event that brings this point to light. I saw a young boy, probably 3 or 4 years old holding the hand of his father while watching a parade. The boy started clapping and jumping up and down with joy as a float approached. The father looked down at him and said, very sternly: "Don't cheer for this float, they are not our team. Our team's float will come later." It was so shocking to me, and yet all too familiar. We often, unconsciously, teach our children to judge, and to separate from their inherent joy.

If we absorb these concepts and live by them as if they are true we can get stuck in a very painful cycle. What's worse, many of us are taught that not only have we done wrong but that we *are* wrong. We are taught that we are not worthy, and are undeserving. When we believe that there is something essentially wrong with us, something that will never be fixed because it's a part of who we are—that's an incredibly heavy and painful burden to carry. If we hold "I am wrong" as our central self-definition, how can we thrive? How can we nurture healthy relationships? How can we experience the joy that is our birthright?

The tendency is to numb the very real pain that comes from this self-identity. And, using drugs, alcohol or other addictive behaviors is an effective way to do this, at least initially. Another tendency is to search for external validation, to strive to show the world a different face than the one we believe we have. "If only I can act good enough or be successful enough, then maybe people won't notice how awful I really am." We try to hide the central "truth" about our brokenness; we live a lie. And that too, is a terrible burden to live with. It's no wonder we find ourselves trapped in addictive behaviors. Addiction has been called "the great ache" that we are trying to soothe and fix from the outside in.

I discovered drugs and alcohol when I was fourteen. And, at the time, it felt like a great and awesome discovery! When I took that drink, I relaxed for the first time in seven years. I often hear people say that when they started drinking or using drugs they felt better-looking, smarter, or more on top of things. I don't know if I felt any of that, but I do remember feeling immense relief—a numbness—like all the things that made me feel "wrong" just didn't matter anymore. I felt relief from the disconnection that I was experiencing, and some relief from that excruciating pain that was at the core of my life's perspective.

Drugs and alcohol were more than a relief for me; they saved my life, and I suppose if they had continued to work for me I might have never gotten sober. In truth, if drugs and alcohol continued to work the way they did in the beginning, I would possibly still be using them. We all look for ways to cope with difficult circumstances, and for many people, drugs and alcohol are one such coping mechanism. I think it helps to look at these coping mechanisms not so much as bad or wrong choices but as brilliant strategies. Even though drinking and using drugs didn't give me the lasting healing I was longing for, they were actually a brilliant strategy, because they literally saved my life. Without them I think I could have snapped in some way; the core false beliefs I had picked up, such as "I'm worthless" and "The world is a dangerous place"—were too overwhelming otherwise.

I believe, in retrospect, that this period in my life was a low-level search for spiritual connection. In other words, I was seeking to fill the inner emptiness by grabbing something outside of myself to gain relief. It was as though I had my umbilical cord in my hand and was trying to find a place to "plug in." I felt there was something wrong with me, and I was looking outside myself for a fix, a cure, a source of relief from the sense of spiritual bankruptcy that I was experiencing. You see, I have come to understand that drugs and alcohol were never the problem. They were a solution to something that felt broken within.

Drinking and using drugs worked for me for awhile, and I drank from the age of 14 until I was 20. But what started out as a brilliant strategy eventually stopped working. What once helped me to feel a sense of connection eventually led to me feeling more and more disconnected. And so, in June of 1986, when I was just fifty-two days away from my twenty-first birthday, I got clean and sober. That was the beginning of an incredible spiritual journey. I've been blessed with continuous sobriety ever since, and now have over thirty years clean and sober. I'm eternally grateful for that because it has been the foundation of a new life and a new way of being.

When I first got sober, I was incredibly rigid, incredibly afraid and shut down. I was trying everything I could to control the *externals* of my life because I felt so out of control *internally*. Without the drugs and alcohol to help me cope with the experience of emptiness and disconnection, I began, once more, to experience all the fear and alienation, all the judgment that had driven me to drink in the first place. Ever since I was a young child I had created a life based on a set of false beliefs and perspectives. I believed that I was broken, and I had been attracting people who seemed to be confirming that belief. In other words, I had created my external life based on internal, fundamental lies about myself and the world.

Fortunately for me, two things happened to direct me on the path to sustained recovery. Soon after I got sober, I met a remarkable woman named Mary Helen Brownell. She was the most enlightened being I had ever met. There was a magical quality about her that I had never experienced before. In her gentle and loving way, Mary Helen introduced me to a new way of being, which wasn't about looking outside myself for validation, but about embarking on an inward journey, looking first at what I needed to unlearn and release.

Then, in 1988, two years into my recovery, I walked into a Unity Church, and the trajectory of my life was changed once again. I became a spiritual seeker. Eventually, I traveled to southern India to stay and study at the ashram of "the hugging guru" Sri Mata Amritanandamayi Devi, known as Amma, or Mother. I studied both Eastern and Western philosophy and religion extensively during those early years. I developed a meditation practice, and I continued to use metaphysical spiritual principles to wake up to a new way of living. I deepened my recovery and felt more and more grounded in the truth of my being.

But my journey did not follow a straight line. Around the age of 30, I reached a point in my spiritual life that called for deeper inner clearing, but I hesitated. Rather than stepping forward and doing the work, I pulled back. I moved into reverse. I once again became outer-focused. Egoism snuck into my recovery and I began to forget the importance of my spiritual practice; I began to forget what was truly important to me, which was maintaining a connection with Source (or love, or light, or whatever word you use). I went back to outer seeking, but this time it wasn't with drugs or alcohol. This time my addiction was to success and achievement.

I had always grappled with money and longed to advance my social status. I knew people with money and privilege, and I wanted what they had. I believed if I just got the perfect house, the perfect car, and the perfect partner, all would be OK, and I would be OK. And now, with ten years of sobriety under my belt, I was ready to "manifest" what I believed was the life of my dreams. I opened a furniture business that soon became very successful. I moved into a two-bedroom home in San Francisco, with a big deck on the hill overlooking the Castro. It was decorated with designer furniture, original artwork by well-known artists, and perfect lighting. I got the new charcoal-colored Lexus; I went to the big Gold's gym in the Castro and worked to perfect my body. It was as if I, once again, had my umbilical cord in my hand trying to find something outside of myself to plug into and fix something that felt broken within.

Interestingly enough, I took the metaphysical principles I had long been studying and shifted them to fit my outward-looking search. I misinterpreted these principles and truths, and heard them through my egoistic lens rather than exploring the deeper meaning. When I heard people saying, "Thoughts held in mind produce after their kind," I interpreted that to mean that if I used affirmations in the "right" way, I would amass more material possessions. I believed if I was "spiritual enough" I could create the life of my dreams. I started to believe that the metaphysical principles of manifestation were *only* about creating the perfect life on the outside.

But as a friend of mine says, "Using affirmations without doing the deeper inner work is like putting icing on stale bread and calling it cake." Sadly, but not surprisingly, I still held onto my own stories of essential brokenness. I still felt, deep down, that I couldn't make it, that if people knew me they would judge me and leave me. So, I didn't share myself, not authentically at least. I didn't tell anyone, not even my boyfriend, what was going on inside; with him, as with everyone around me, everything was "fine." I felt like a fraud.

Instead of doing the necessary deeper inner work, I slipped into an old pattern, now camouflaged to fit my new identity as a spiritual person. I didn't have the tools to deal with my external success. The more successful I became, the more I believed I needed to acquire. I felt emptier and emptier and lost contact with my essential nature. The trajectory of my life took me way off course, and I found myself isolated and afraid once again.

In 2004, I first heard the calling to go into ministry. Every time I was at Unity, I felt this inner knowing and desire to become a minister and spiritual teacher. For a good year, I said no to that calling, because I had created a life that seemed to be incredibly successful in the outer realm, and I didn't understand how I could possibly shift into ministry and let go of what I thought was the life of my dreams. I didn't understand that my inner vision would lead to the true life of my dreams. Finally, I spoke my desire to go into ministry out loud. I began my formal ministerial and spiritual counseling training in 2005. Once I began this process, my inner life began to open up in beautiful ways. My outer life began to crumble.

There's a wonderful concept in metaphysical teachings called "chemicalization," which is when our consciousness evolves to a point beyond our current level, and our material world crumbles as a result. What can happen is a lot of difficulty, because the old way gets "burned off" in order for us to step fully into this new consciousness. That was certainly my experience. In retrospect, I can see that this happened because I had built my life on a very shaky foundation, and saying yes to this higher vision for my life required the old paradigm to collapse. As I continued taking classes toward ordination, my world continued to fall apart.

My business collapsed and the debt I had incurred caught up with me. I owed people money; the rumor mill was going nuts;

friends were walking away. It felt like a nightmare, and it was, from one perspective. I kept going to classes, kept listening to the calling, but I still could not let go of my outer-directed vision. I started another business, thinking, "This time it will be different." It was not. Same story, same outcome. I had a falling out with my business partner, and then I lost the second business, even more dramatically than the first.

"What we resist persists." I had been hearing this for years, I knew it in my head. So why was it so difficult for me to stop resisting the call to a deeper inner life? We are taught from a very early age a specific vision of what strength looks like and what weakness is, and what many of us learn is pretty much the opposite of the truth. The willingness to be vulnerable, to genuinely let others see us, to be capable of true intimacy—we are often taught that these are weaknesses. Strength, we learn, is having all the answers, figuring things out, and using force to get what we think we need. Strength is hiding your brokenness in the "stuff" of external success.

My core false beliefs were very deeply rooted in my unconscious, so it makes sense that my spiritual growth and recovery took time. I needed not only to unlearn the false beliefs, but to learn the true power and courage of flowing with life, of letting go, of being present. And to learn this, I needed to experience it, and I needed to deepen my spiritual practice. At that point, I resisted it, even though I knew it was important. I played hide-and-seek with the truth, with Source.

One such deepening experience happened some years ago when I traveled to India. Varanasi, in northern India, is said to be the oldest continuously inhabited city in the world. Built along the western banks of the Ganges River, it is a pilgrimage site for thousands upon thousands, who believe that if you die and are cremated there, your karma will be removed and you will achieve nirvana, and be released from this physical realm. This is where I found myself in 2006, on a spiritual quest with about thirty other seekers.

In the oldest parts of the city, roads are too narrow for cars, so we entered the city by bicycle rickshaw. I could feel the spiritual energy intensifying as we moved along the twisting streets, popping with colors, crowded with people, cows, and vehicles of every sort. A chill went up my arms, and my heart began to open. Once we reached the oldest part of the city, we were escorted to the river on foot by twin boys, about twelve years old. They had short dark hair and no shoes, and they wore simple, plain colored dhoti. Both were deaf. Their gentle energies were incredibly striking. In the midst of all the chaos of the city, they had a wordless presence—kindness and love shone in their eyes as they gently helped us get to our destination.

By the time we reached the river, it was getting to be dusk. We all got in a boat and pushed out onto the water. Looking back at the river bank, we could see the places where people bathe, perform ceremonies, and cremate the dead. We were just in time for the Ganga Aarti, the festival of lights, which happens every evening at sundown on the main Ghat, the Dashashwamedh. Light, singing, bells, incense, movement—all came together to pay tribute to the mighty Ganges and the spirits of the departed. All around us, lights floated on the water. And all along the river, the cremation fires burned. As I settled in, a profound peace entered my body and, in that moment, my ego seemed to be stripped away. Suddenly, I knew there was no separation, no us and them, no place where I ended and someone else began. There was no good, no bad, no right or wrong, and there was no judgment. I knew I could at last let go. I began to sob. It felt like years of trauma and sadness were being washed away.

Suddenly, the electrical power went out and shrouded half

of the city in darkness (not uncommon in many parts of India). The only things that lit up the night sky were the ceremonial lights and the fires of cremation. Our guides quietly steered the boat until we were just a few feet away from one of the Ghats, and there we sat for what seemed like an eternity, watching the funeral ceremonies. The flames filled up the otherwise dark night with beautiful, sparkling light. The experience of my sudden awakening lasted with the same intensity for several hours. I awoke the next morning to discover my life had permanently shifted into a new way of being.

Since that experience, my ego has continued to make its appearance in my life, but that moment allowed me to have a permanent change in my relationship *with* my ego. My ego has not died, I simply changed the way I see it and the way it plays a role in my life. In other words, I was restored to the truth of who and what I am, which is one with Spirit. From that moment, my life has been filled with more love, more connection, more joy, and more happiness than I knew possible.

It's not that I always had it easy after my experience in India. In fact, after I returned home my life, in many ways, became more challenging, at least in the short term. The difference was that I was able make the commitment to doing the inner work, to dedicate myself to the spiritual practices that this effort requires. Over time, I could see and accept that my life's work is to joyfully share this experience of my awakening, to share my own journey of moving through darkness and into light so that others can experience their own light and love. And once I got clear on what was mine to do, the outer circumstances of my life began to fall into place. I discovered that spending time in the silence, staying true to my inner calling, and taking conscious actions were tools that allowed my dreams and visions to naturally manifest in the outer realm.

Here's how it looked: I continued to answer my calling to

the ministry, serving as the Ministerial Associate at Unity San Francisco while continuing my studies. Around that same time, I started working in the addiction treatment field as a spiritual counselor. In my addiction work, I created and implemented a full-scale spiritual care program within a residential treatment program. My experience from the beginning of that effort was that people were hungry for a spiritual approach to their recovery that guided them to break free from the cycle of addictive behavior and return to a place of peace and happiness. This was very exciting for me, as it seemed to be just what I was meant to do.

In 2012, I founded the Awakened Living Spiritual Center, which was given the distinct honor of being selected by Michael Bernard Beckwith to become Agape Bay Area: A Center for Awakened Living in 2017. Agape Bay Area is a twenty-first century movement for people who consider themselves spiritual explorers, and have a deep hunger for personal and global transformation. My book *Conscious Being: Awakening to Your True Nature* was published in the spring of 2015. *Conscious Being* is an insightful guide for rediscovering your essential nature and living an intentional and awakened life. Today, I am truly living the life of my dreams. I am the founding minister of Agape Bay Area in Oakland, and I am privileged to speak to audiences around the world about spiritual awakening and addiction recovery. I am also blessed to work at several top-tier treatment programs, where I facilitate groups based on *The Conscious Recovery Method*TM I created. *The Conscious Recovery Method* offers a way to disrupt addictive behavior through the practice of the metaphysical and mystical principles we will be exploring in this book. Additionally, I am the host of *Conscious Being Radio*. All of this has manifested in my life because I have trusted my inner knowing. I have dedicated myself to spending time in silence and taking conscious action based on the internal messages I have received through vision. What I have discovered to be true is that this is not only possible for us all, it is our divine birthright.

Internally, I have also experienced a tremendous transformation, which took many years and included some seemingly sudden shifts—from resistance and fear to openness and presence. And, the greatest paradox is, once I released the expectation that I *needed* my outer life to look a certain way in order to be OK, my outer life started to manifest with a greater abundance than ever before. Once I surrendered my egoic structure (the old beliefs that kept me feeling stuck and limited) and became clear on my inner purpose, my outer circumstances aligned with my inner knowing. Life seems to work that way. My experience has shown me that when we do our inner work of awakening, when we learn to flow with life instead of resisting it, we can enter into a life filled with love, gratitude and joy. Additionally, as more and more of us are waking up to this and committing to practicing spiritual principles, it has a ripple effect on the collective as well; on politics, on the health of the planet, on everything.

We do have a choice in how we view the world. All those early decisions we make, all the ideas we carry around that keep us small and keep us limited—we can take responsibility for those and let them go. We can experience oneness. Because love is the ultimate truth of who we are, peace is the deepest truth of who we are. We can restore the innate knowing we had as children, and together we can facilitate a continuation of the awakening that is already underway on this planet. This is what I wish for you. If you are in one of those periods of darkness, or if you are struggling with addiction in any form, you can also have this incredible life filled with joy and connection.

My sincere hope is that working though this book will be helpful to you along the way.

Introduction

THE ADDICTED SELF

Every addiction arises from an unconscious refusal to face and move through your own pain. Every addiction starts with pain and ends with pain. Whatever the substance you are addicted to — alcohol, food, legal or illegal drugs, or a person — you are using something or somebody to cover up your pain.

— *Eckhart Tolle*

What is Conscious Recovery?

The purpose of *Conscious Recovery* is to offer a spiritual perspective that can assist you in addressing the underlying root causes of your addictive behaviors. It is intended to enhance any program, therapy, or other support system in which you are currently engaged. Its aim is *not* to provide definitive answers, but to introduce questions that can assist you in accessing your own inner wisdom and rediscover your true nature. You are your own best teacher, and you hold the key to ending your own suffering. *Conscious Recovery* can assist you in deepening your understanding of addiction, provide you a roadmap toward liberation, and offer tools to assist you in living your most dynamic and connected life.

Conscious Recovery is not written like a novel and is not intended to be read like one. It is designed to be "worked through" slowly. My encouragement is that you take your time in reading this book.

I imagine some of you have been in recovery for a while, maybe even a long time, and you have learned a good deal about yourself, about your addiction, and about your relationships. Maybe you still value participating in your support groups, but it seems that what you get out of them has changed. Maybe you've achieved physical sobriety, but there is a longing for something deeper. Maybe you feel stronger and more resilient overall, and now you're looking for a different kind of growth. Or maybe you've tried traditional recovery methods and they don't seem to work for you. You want to shift your addictive behavior, but you don't believe you are powerless over it; you don't want to call yourself an addict and you don't understand the need to. If you resonate with any of this, *Conscious Recovery* may be the book for you, as it offers a spiritual perspective that can assist you in breaking free from addictive behavior.

Let's start by looking at how that perspective fits in with what you may have already experienced in your recovery. Then we'll look at the root causes of addiction through the spiritual lens, and explore the promise of a fresh approach to recovery. I firmly believe that this approach will help you move from a life of separation, a life of fear, a life of addiction, to a life in which you deeply recognize your oneness with Spirit. And finally, I'll explain what *Conscious Recovery* offers you; how the book is organized and the spiritual practices it teaches for your journey toward wholeness.

Let's start with one of those practices: an affirmation.

I am a perfect expression of love.

I now invite you to take a moment and go within. Wherever you are, take this opportunity to tap into the deep wellspring of your own inner wisdom. Try to connect with your inner essence and recognize your oneness with Source. Wherever you are, I'd like you to repeat: *I am a perfect expression of love.*

The Room of Spirit

"Everyone is a house with four rooms, a physical, a mental, an emotional and a spiritual. Most of us tend to live in one room most of the time, but unless we go into every room, every day, even if only to keep it aired, we are not a complete person." - Indian Proverb

In the physical room is your relationship with your body and its interaction with the physical world. The mental room houses your thoughts and ideas, the assumptions and expectations that shape your perspective of the world. The emotional room is the seat of feelings, and for some, it can be a place to avoid, or run from. The spiritual room is where you connect with your innermost self, and with Source that lies within all reality. Part of your healing journey is coming to recognize the importance of all four rooms, and spending time in each of them to strengthen your whole being.

If you have been in recovery for any length of time, you know that addiction can be considered from any of these rooms. All four: the physical, the mental, the emotional, and the spiritual, are present in any addiction, and they can be utilized in your recovery. Most commonly contemplated, perhaps, is the physical approach to recovery, with its attention to the physical symptoms of addiction and physical healing (e.g., the disease model, studying brain chemistry and genetics, considering medications, changing diet and exercise patterns, and so on). People in recovery also spend time in the mental and emotional rooms, with help from therapists, sponsors, and support groups. Living in all four of these rooms can bring us a long way along the road to recovery.

But as the proverb tells us: "*Most of us tend to live in one room*

3

most of the time." Often neglected in recovery work is the spiritual room, from which we can consider the spiritual questions involved in recovery: What is the root cause of addiction? What is the underlying condition of fragmentation and disconnection that leads people to addiction and addictive behaviors? How can sitting in the room of Spirit bring us to a place of deeper healing and peace?

My training and experience has led me to look at addiction through the spiritual lens. I'm blessed to have spent the past decade working with the spiritual aspects of addiction and recovery. I have seen firsthand how a spiritual perspective can build on and integrate with the physical, mental, and emotional approaches. I have witnessed the healing power of metaphysical and mystical spiritual principles and practices, and experienced how this perspective can assist you in entering more deeply into your recovery, connecting you more fully with Spirit and with others.

One thing I've noticed in my years of working in the field of addiction recovery is that addiction treatment often focuses on symptoms rather than root causes. We tend to see addiction as a problem and then look for a way to *solve* that problem. There is nothing inherently wrong with this approach—we certainly do need to address symptoms and behaviors, and there is a point in the recovery process where it's important to acknowledge your powerlessness in order to change your behavior. But that's not all there is to it, and to think it is sufficient doesn't address addiction from all four rooms. So, my intention for this book is to broaden your viewpoint by addressing not only the symptoms, but also the root causes of addiction. Then we'll examine more deeply the spiritual principles and practices that will enable you to break free from the addictive cycle.

Of course, the four rooms are not cut off from one another; they are all part of the same house, connected by doorways and hallways. We are integrated beings, and addressing the spiritual aspects of addiction will bring us into the other rooms, especially the rooms of thought and emotion. Coming from a spiritual perspective will enable us to take the insights of the physical, the mental, and the emotional rooms to a new place, a place of integration and wholeness.

This book is for you if your recovery is bringing up questions that are not fully answered in the physical room, the mental room, the emotional room. This book is for you if are looking for a spiritual path, or to deepen the spiritual path you are on. This book is for you if you work as a clinician in the addiction treatment field and you want to look more deeply at the root causes of addiction, and you want to offer your clients tools for addressing those root causes. This book is for you if your feelings of responsibility for your clients is exhausting you and you're looking for a way to detach without losing empathy or compassion.

Conscious Recovery is not intended to be a recovery "program" that stands on its own. It is intended to enhance the work you are already doing and the support you are already getting. It's not an either/or proposition. It is not suggesting that you abandon the physical, mental, or emotional approaches. Indeed, I encourage you to remain grounded in the other rooms—work with your doctor, therapist, sponsor, and support network. At the same time, I invite you now to nourish and enhance the work you do in those rooms by joining me in considering recovery from a spiritual perspective.

The Outer-Focused Life

When we look at addiction, we might automatically think of dependence on drugs or alcohol. We might imagine a person who is utterly down and out, someone who has lost their job and their relationships and is destitute and homeless. While that is indeed one face of addiction, the definition I'd like to work with is much broader.

Many of us live with a sense of emptiness or disconnection. We feel broken and empty inside, and we look outside ourselves for a solution. Or we're uncomfortable with what we see when we look within. If we cannot bear to be with our self, to look at that inner "edge" where our darkest feelings and memories reside, then we may turn outward for something that will seem to pull us back to safety. In any case, the pain of what's inside causes us to look outside for relief. Now, that outward-seeking might not in itself be an addiction. But as we look elsewhere to fix what feels broken, empty or uncomfortable inside, we can begin to depend on those outside sources to feel safe or whole. When we use an external solution repetitively so that it becomes a habit for us, a need, then we're developing an addiction. From this perspective, addiction fits the Buddhist concept of aversion (to pain) and clinging (to relief).

So, addiction can be viewed simply as the outer-focused life. Rather than doing the inner work of healing that which feels broken or meaningless, we focus on something outside of ourselves to resolve, numb, or avoid a sense of psychic pain. And it's a solution that can work for a long time. Our solution can be drugs and alcohol, but it can also be other things. We can be dependent on our own thoughts, using them as a strategy for resolving or alleviating our inner conflict. We can be addicted to ideas, to other people, even to our recovery program. We can use religion, focusing on the idea that there's a God up there, or a set of laws, and if we can just surrender ourselves to these, then everything will be OK. For example, one phrase that is commonly heard in recovery circles is: "We have a God-shaped hole inside of us." The meaning of this is that we are walking around with a sense of inner emptiness that only God can fill. I want to offer a different perspective here. Saying that God needs to "fill" this hole is still an addictive thought. What if, rather than imagining that it needs to be filled, we can learn to walk with it, and "be" with it in the world? This is how we can shift from looking for something or someone *else* to ease the pain, and begin to integrate and accept our felt sense of inner emptiness. This is how we can learn to be with ourselves in a new and more accepting way.

What all these strategies have in common within the context of addiction is that they all serve to relieve some of the agony that comes from an inner sense of fragmentation and unease, a sense that we don't fit, that we are "wrong" in the world.

The Roots of Addiction

Where does this sense of brokenness and emptiness, which addiction tries to fix, come from? The roots of addiction can be considered from all four of the rooms in our human house. In the physical room, we can consider chemical imbalances, genetic propensities, or depression. In the mental room, we can consider the ideas and assumptions that lead us to feel alienated and disconnected. An emotional perspective can lead us into our personal stories, where we might find injuries to our psyches that have left us with overwhelming feelings.

The spiritual perspective does not disregard these insights. Rather it adds to them the wisdom of all the spiritual viewpoint, which tells us that human suffering stems from a loss of connection with the truth of who and what we are. The truth is that we are fundamentally whole and perfect. We are one with Source, one with Spirit, one with love. We'll be sitting with this truth a good deal throughout the book, so I won't go very deeply into it here. Let me simply say that by "fundamentally" I am not referring to the sense of self that we present to the world. I am not referring to the persona, the personality, or the ego. The true self is the essential self which lives in the midst of those things, the self that is unharmed and unharmable, one with divinity—the core of who we are. The truth is that we are fundamentally impeccable and unflawed.

If this sounds foreign to you, you're not alone. Very often we simply do not experience the world in this way; for a variety of reasons we see ourselves as anything but whole and perfect. We have learned things from an early age that tell us we are broken, that life is a struggle, that we have no choice. These false beliefs thus separate us from the truth of who we are, and this forgetting, this sense of brokenness and alienation, is extremely painful. Addictive behavior and patterns are a response to that pain and a search for relief.

Cultural Influences

How do we lose sight of the truth of who we are? From where do we get this belief in our own brokenness, fragmentation, and limitation? The answer lies all around us. We live in a culture that's addicted to the concepts of "right" and "wrong," highly addicted to competition, highly addicted to the belief in "us" and "them." We live in a world where there is suffering and pain, and our society doesn't offer many healthy tools for dealing with that. And, depending on the specific culture where we are raised, we may get many layers of messages that teach us we are fundamentally broken or damaged in some way. Even if we had a stable and loving upbringing and are blessed with a safe and nurturing environment, we are still bombarded by messages that run counter to the truth of our fundamental perfection. In addition, many of us are burdened by unresolved trauma and toxic shame, which only compound the beliefs that are downloaded from our culture. We become fragmented; our sense of self shatters and is lost.

All of these things are involved in creating a point of view we might call "victim consciousness," which says, quite simply, that things happen *to* us. We believe we have little control over what happens; other people and forces outside ourselves determine our life. In this victim consciousness, addiction runs rampant. That's because if we believe the solution is outside of us, we are going to cling to all sorts of externals, all sorts of different strategies, to try to relieve that psychic pain. Although those strategies can work for us for a period of time, they tend to become addictive, to lose their efficacy and they ultimately start to work against us.

Holistic and Integrated Recovery

How do we break free from the addictive self? Just as there is a spiritual aspect to addiction, so there is a spiritual aspect to recovery. A holistic and integrative recovery acknowledges and utilizes the power that resides in all four rooms of the human experience: the physical, the mental, the emotional, and the spiritual.

The physical room gives us the insight that addiction is a disease, and working from that insight has offered us many powerful tools and approaches. I have benefitted from these insights and tools in my own recovery, but I am not an addiction medicine physician or a psychiatrist. So, I will leave the physical to these health care professionals, and encourage you again to enter this room regularly.

Moving on through the rooms: The mental room gives us the insight that our thoughts and ideas, our assumptions and our worldview, have an enormous role in both addiction and recovery. We will be entering this room often as we progress through *Conscious Recovery*. And the room of the emotions shows us that how we respond to our feelings—whether we are overcome by them, disengage from them, or somewhere in between—is a factor in our addiction. Healing emotional trauma and acknowledging our dependence on old emotional patterns can be a large part of recovery. This room is also one that we will visit throughout this book.

My training and expertise, and I suppose my temperament, have led me to focus my attention on the room of Spirit and what it teaches us about addiction and recovery. What this room reveals is that addiction stems from fragmentation; it is a strategy for dealing with the pain of disconnection from our essential self. When we reframe our approach to addiction in this way, we can see that the underlying problem is not the addiction. The problem beneath the symptoms of addiction is spiritual and psychic disconnection, the fragmentation of self. Recognizing this allows us to start to identify and let go of core beliefs, to let go of those solutions that are no longer working, and to move toward a place of wholeness and perfection.

Thus begins this incredible voyage inward. On this journey, we are not looking for something independent of ourselves, we are turning inward and recognizing that this pathway can lead us to return to the essential self. The spiritual perspective allows us to make an important internal shift. When we move from an outer-focused life to an inner-focused way of being, we can start to recognize and engage our wholeness, our inherent perfection. And when we are willing to look within and do the work of inner clearing, removing the false ideas, perspectives, and stories we have about our lives, we can open to this new way of being.

Getting the Most Out of Conscious Recovery

In *Conscious Recovery*, I will help you approach addiction from an integrative, spiritual perspective. After describing and explaining addiction's spiritual roots, this book will guide you through methods of breaking the cycle of your addictive behavior, and into an experience of your inherent wholeness, thereby helping you to find a deeper sense of purpose and connection in your life.

Conscious Recovery is organized into three parts.

Part 1, "The Roots of Addiction," delves further into the three spiritual root causes of addiction and addictive behavior: unresolved trauma in all its various forms (Chapter 1), the fragmentation of the self that can generate and develop core false beliefs (Chapter 2), and toxic shame, which is a pervasive and corrosive sense of self that further separates you from your true nature (Chapter 3).

Part 2, "Breaking the Cycle of Addiction," introduces the inner work involved in interrupting compulsive patterns, so you can reconnect with your deepest truth. This work includes creating safety through openness, spiritual community, and conscious awareness (Chapter 4), unlearning your core false beliefs, habits and points of view (Chapter 5), and discovering powerful spiritual principles that, when practiced, can allow you to permanently break free from your addictive tendencies (Chapter 6).

Part 3, "A Return to Wholeness," will explore how you can move your life from power-less to power-full (Chapter 7), how you can return to the essential wholeness of your divine nature (Chapter 8), and finally, how you can live an awakened and purpose-filled life (Chapter 9).

As you work through this book, keep in mind that the spiritual approach is not an exact science. Developing the inner life is not always a straightforward, linear process. It can even sometimes be a painful process that calls us to be patient with ourselves as we shift our perspectives, let go of old ways of thinking and living, and deepen in awareness. That said, there is a pattern to it; it's a route taken by countless people before us. What I am offering here is a guidebook on that spiritual path.

PART 1

THE ROOTS OF ADDICTION

Your essential self is perfection. You are essentially
one with Source, or love, or light—whatever
word you use for divinity. Even before you knew
language, you came into this world with absolute
connection to the ultimate power of the universe.

This is a core truth. It's the truth we are born with, the
truth that makes us whole, gives us a sense of connection,
a sense of peace and harmony. But in the process of
living we often forget this core truth, and we lose our
balance. We lose sight of who and what we truly are.

In Part 1 of this book we will consider how that happens.
We'll consider how addictive behavior works in the context
of our search for love and connection. We'll look at the
root causes of our addictive behavior: unresolved trauma,
spiritual disconnection, and toxic shame. And we'll start
to examine what we can do when our addictive behavior no
longer serves us, when it becomes compulsive and begins to
hurt us and close us off further from what we truly seek.

Chapter One
UNRESOLVED TRAUMA

During our early life we began making agreements. Our parents rewarded us when we did what they wanted and they punished us when we didn't. We also learned behaviors and habits in school, church, and from other adults and children on the playground. The tools of reward and punishment were often emotional and sometimes physical. The impact of other people's opinions and reactions to us became a very strong force in the habits we created. In this process we created agreements in our mind of who we should be, what we shouldn't be, who we were, and who we were not. Over time we learned to live our life based on the agreements in our own mind. We learned to live according to the agreements that came from the opinion of others. In this process of domestication, it turns out that the choices we make and the life we live is more driven by the opinions we learned from others than one we would choose on our own.
— Don Miguel Ruiz, The Four Agreements

What Is Unresolved Trauma?

The word "trauma" can bring to mind certain ideas or associations. War zones may come to mind, or serious accidents, or the loss of someone close to you, or childhood abuse. You may have read about research on the physical, mental, and emotional impacts of PTSD (Posttraumatic Stress Disorder) on returning soldiers and victims of abuse, and maybe you've experienced some of those impacts yourself. But we don't often hear about the spiritual effects of trauma, or about how a spiritual perspective can help us heal. When you begin to uncover the roots of your addiction, very often you find unresolved trauma. In this chapter, I invite you to take a spiritual approach to your unresolved trauma, to connect with your innermost self and unveil the spiritual source of your suffering.

In her book, *The Trauma Tool Kit: Healing PTSD from the Inside Out*, Susan P. Bannit provides the following definition of trauma: "*Traumatic events by definition overwhelm our ability to cope. When the mind becomes flooded with emotion, a circuit breaker is thrown that allows us to survive the experience fairly intact. That is, without becoming psychotic or frying out one of the brain centers. The cost of this blown circuit is emotion frozen within the body. In other words, we often unconsciously stop feeling our trauma part way into it, like a movie that is still going after the sound has been turned off. We cannot heal until we move fully through that trauma, including all of the feelings of that event.*" Trauma is something that overwhelms our ability to cope. And unresolved trauma continues to hurt us because we are stuck in the traumatic experience.

Let's explore this more deeply. You've probably heard of "fight or flight," right? Those are the body's reactions to danger, and in the moment of trauma, when the body is flooded with adrenaline, those are its strategies for coping. But when the experience is overwhelming, there's a third survival strategy: to freeze. When we freeze, we detach, we leave the room, we lock away whatever part of the experience is most threatening to us. We stop being present to the traumatic experience. This is also called dissociation.

Dissociation can get us through the immediate trauma,

but unfortunately, that "frozen emotion" can get trapped in the body, resulting in all kinds of ill effects over time. Someone who experiences repeated physical abuse growing up, for example, can experience a psychological and a spiritual impact that gets stored in the body and remains there long after the obvious physical damage is healed. If we've gone numb often enough in response to abuse or injury, numbness becomes a habit. And it's a dangerous habit, because the pain and suffering are still there, stuck in our bodies. Walking around with that kind of unresolved pain is a root cause of addiction. If the trauma that's trapped in our body gets reactivated every time we hear a certain sound or see a certain person, if things in our everyday life can retrigger that powerful fight, flight, or freeze response—that can make it incredibly hard to function. So, we may turn to things that help us cope, like addictive substances or behaviors.

Before we get too far into the consequences of trauma, let's examine how the different types of trauma—physical, mental, emotional, spiritual, and vicarious—can wound us long after the initial event, and how that can lead to an addicted life. As we discuss these different types of trauma, remember that our physical, emotional, mental, and spiritual selves are not in fact separate; these categories are just constructs to help us understand.

Physical Trauma

Physical trauma encompasses many different experiences, including physical abuse, domestic violence, assault, self-injury, natural disaster, an automobile accident, or battlefield trauma, to name a few. Medically speaking, physical trauma is a severe injury to the body, whatever the cause. The way an individual responds to physical trauma depends on the level of trauma as well as on their individual resiliency and support systems. Let's look at a few of the possible responses to and the effects of physical trauma.

To begin with, it's not uncommon for some of the physical and emotional responses to shut down during trauma. Many people, for example, report feeling no physical pain in the moments after a traumatic injury—the pain centers of the brain simply stop registering pain levels. In the longer term, physical trauma can also have consequences beyond the initial injury, including shock, loss of organ function, infection and sepsis, and even a disruption of genetic functioning. Then there's the impact of the life-saving treatments we might undergo after the trauma, which can themselves be very distressing. Long-term emotional responses to physical trauma can include anxiety, flashbacks, unpredictable emotions, and other types of emotional distress.

The way we recover from physical trauma seems to depend in part on how long-standing it is. If you have good support systems and are relatively healthy, you might withstand an intense but short-lived trauma, like being injured in a car accident, with few long-term effects. But a physical trauma that happens over time, such as chronic, long-term physical abuse, neglect, domestic violence, or multiple tours of combat duty, can be more difficult to recover from. This kind of trauma, called "complex trauma," can have very deep psychological and spiritual impacts, including trouble in trusting others, difficulty controlling emotions, behaviors, and higher levels of stress, which in turn can damage the immune system, impede brain development, and result in long-term damage to our emotional and physical health. If we experience this sort of trauma, it's going to affect how we perceive ourselves and our world. Even if the physical wounds are mended, there is a psychological and a spiritual impact that gets stored in the body and is harder to heal. Thus unresolved physical trauma can be a root cause of addiction, because walking around with that kind of pain often leads us to turn to substances and behaviors that ease our suffering, but can also become addictive.

Mental Trauma

It seems that the vast majority of us experience some degree of mental trauma in childhood simply by receiving repeated messages of untruth. This mental trauma can be inflicted by otherwise loving parents, teachers, and other adults who are simply passing down what they themselves were taught as children. As children, most of us learn lies about ourselves and our world instead of the truth of our inherent wholeness. Being taught a worldview that assumes that the world is governed by limitation, fear, separation, or aggression can make us believe, at a fundamental level, that the world is not safe. This mental trauma is an injury to our understanding of the world.

Think for a moment about whether and how this took place as you grew up. I know that most of the adults in my own childhood taught me that the world wasn't fair, that the world wasn't safe and that there was a lot of scarcity. I received both overt and covert messages that I wouldn't amount to anything and might as well just accept a life of limitation. The reason I bring this very common experience into the conversation about trauma is that it is genuinely rather traumatic to be taught something that is so counter to the ultimate truth of our existence. These lies are traumatic. They injure us because they enter our psyches and distort the way we see ourselves. They become our core beliefs, our core *false* beliefs. When we walk around believing things like, "The world is not safe," or "Life is a struggle," or "I'm fundamentally unworthy," then it makes sense to live in a permanent state of fight, flight, or freeze response.

19

When we live in a world that seems unsafe and unloving, there's a tendency to create a safety zone and never move outside of those boundaries. So, we stop growing, because growth only happens when we expand our comfort zone. People who have experienced mental trauma—and again, that's virtually all of us who are here in this human realm—have been taught some sort of lie about their essential nature. For us to expand outside of our comfort zone can often feel disorienting and frightening. This is because we've unconsciously created a safety zone that on one hand seems to keep us feeling safe, but on another hand, keeps us absolutely stuck in limited ways of seeing ourselves.

Emotional Trauma

Emotional trauma can be inflicted by a primary caregiver who is in their own addiction and not able to offer the love and connection we need. It can also come from teachers, ministers, and the like who are still operating from their "woundology," as my friend and colleague Temple Hayes puts it. It can be caused by peers; the proverbial "kid on the playground" acting as a bully. Being repeatedly mocked, insulted, and criticized can make us feel, at a fundamental level, that we are less than, not good enough, and/or unlovable. This is emotional trauma—injury to our emotional well-being.

The following story illustrates how emotional trauma gets stored in our bodies. Some years ago, I was in a motorcycle accident that resulted in me breaking two vertebrae in my upper back. After some healing time had passed, my doctor let me know it was safe to begin getting some deep-tissue massage work done to alleviate the pain I was experiencing. After my first session, my massage therapist let me know that the vertebrae had healed completely, but the muscles around the vertebrae had tightened to protect the vertebrae (even though they no longer actually needed protecting). It was not the

TELEPHONE APPOINTMENT REMINDER

Name: _____AARON K._____

Provider: ___Jackie, NP___

Date: ___10/22___ Time: ___4:40___

Phone Number: ___(650) 471-5296___

Provider will be calling you on the phone number listed above. If this is not the correct number, please check in with secretary at front desk to update.

If you are unable to keep your appointment, please talk to secretary or call (925) 674-4147 to reschedule.

vertebrae that needed to mend, it was now the tightness in the muscles that needed to be "worked out" in order for the pain to be dissipated.

Even though this particular story is about physical trauma, it serves as a metaphor regarding how our psyches can still hold the emotional trauma and hurts from our past. The traumatic event is no longer occurring, but our "freeze" instinct still believes we need protecting. We need to work out the emotional scars associated with the original trauma in order to be free. The spiritual journey, as I hope you're beginning to see, is about reconnecting with your essential truth. You are whole, you are perfect, you are love, and you are loved exactly the way you are.

Spiritual Trauma

Now we move into spiritual trauma, which is very prevalent in our culture and in our world. Spiritual trauma is inflicted when we are not seen as the deepest truth of who and what we are. It is all too common to be taught ideas about ourselves and the world that are counter to this fundamental truth of our being. When we are not seen in this authentic light, we have what is called spiritual disconnection, which is a separation from our essential self. We will be covering this in a more in-depth way in Chapter 2 of this book.

There is a big difference between spirituality and religion. Spirituality is about connection with our essence, and is the deepest truth of what it means to be human. We come into this world with an innate sense of knowing this. We are naturally connected with ourselves, with nature, and with all of life. Religion is an attempt to make sense of spirituality, but all too often, the dogma of religions (rules, tenets, and ideology) create strict guidelines that can cause damage.

Sometimes religion is used to teach us things that don't confirm the ultimate truth of who and what we are. For example, some religions teach the idea of fundamental sin, they teach that we're inherently bad in some way. They teach that only belief in this particular God or practice of this particular religion can save us from our state of fundamental evil. When that message about our fundamental brokenness and dependence is repeated over and over again, when it's illustrated and lived by an authority and an institution that our parents and others around us respect and follow, then it naturally seeps into our spirits and breaks down our relationship with the fundamental truth of who we are. This is spiritual trauma; it is an injury to our spirit.

One tragic consequence of spiritual trauma is a turning away from Spirit. I've seen it countless times. As people grow and learn they begin to come up against the logical inconsistencies in the religious untruths they were taught as children. I have friends who say they woke up one day and realized that 75% of the world didn't follow their religion. They then began to question how a loving God could consign 75% of the world to damnation. This sort of questioning can open us up to spiritual growth. But, all too often, when we encounter these inconsistencies we stop the process cold, and turn away from our spiritual side altogether. This turning away is understandable. For one, the notion of salvation being limited by "correct" belief just doesn't make sense to us anymore. But on a deeper level, the very mention of religion or the slightest experience of Spirit can become a trigger for the religious or spiritual trauma we underwent in our youth. The trauma has so affected our outlook that we can see no way to be spiritual in life.

Vicarious Trauma

I often work with clients who say they have not experienced trauma in their lives, but upon further investigation, they begin to recognize that they have experienced what is called vicarious trauma. Vicarious trauma, simply put, is witnessing a traumatic event or ongoing trauma perpetrated on someone else. This can be witnessing a horrific accident, or seeing someone physically, mentally, emotionally, or spiritually abused once or over an extended period of time. This type of trauma can sometimes gets overlooked, because someone might say a variation of "But, he never abused me," or "I only saw it happen, I was not hurt." The truth is, this type of trauma can be very agonizing because there might be multiple layers to the experience. For example, someone might carry guilt or shame because they were not able to prevent the accident, or they believe they "should have" done something to stop the violence. One example of this is when children witness one parent abusing the other one. These incidents can leave very profound wounds that need to be addressed in order to find resolution and freedom from vicarious trauma.

The Consequences of Unresolved Trauma

As you can see, all types of trauma: physical, mental, emotional, spiritual, and vicarious, lead us back to a distressing separation from our essential self, a false sense that we are inherently broken in some way. Let's look further at some of the consequences of this ongoing injury.

As the earlier story explained, trauma lives in our bodies. If we have unresolved trauma, the responses of fight, flight, or freeze, which are very hard on our nervous systems, can be triggered by everyday physical experiences, and over time this chronic stress takes a toll on our bodies and spirits in addition to the direct physical effect of the trauma. Trauma can take up residence in the body, in effect reinjuring us each time it's activated. It also has been linked to multiple physical diseases.

Whether it's physical, mental, emotional, or spiritual injury

23

that we experience, unresolved trauma can result in a sense that something is fundamentally wrong or broken. And that feeling can get buried deep in the subconscious (the part of our psyche that is not easily accessible to the conscious mind). Let's say you believe that there is something fundamentally wrong with you. You have a core false belief that you're not lovable. What are you going to do? How are you going to respond to this reality? If you're walking around with the unconscious or subconscious belief that you're not lovable, you may very well try to find all sorts of experiences to counter that. You may be become addicted to relationships, love, or sex. You are searching for something outside of yourself to try to undo the core false belief that you're not lovable.

But, quite often, what happens is the opposite. The feeling tone that you hold about yourself is what actually creates what you call reality. So, even though on the surface you may be grabbing for and striving for all sorts of experiences in order to feel love, you're still holding a vibration or a belief about yourself as unlovable. The deeply held feeling tone that you're not lovable works on an unconscious level to attract people who only confirm that negative core false belief. Conversely, you also may tend to be attracted to these very people, in a kind of self-sabotaging reinforcement of those false beliefs.

Trauma and the Unconscious

At Agape Bay Area, our spiritual community in Oakland, we are blessed with a wonderful musician, a beautiful spirit whose contributions to our community are immense. She grew up in the segregated South, and one of the rules of segregation she experienced as a child was that she could not be on the sidewalk at the same time as a white person. If she was walking along and saw a white person coming toward her, she would have to step off the sidewalk and let that person pass. This experience, repeated over and over again, in addition to all of the other experiences of racism and segregation she underwent, entered into her on a physical, mental, emotional, and spiritual level, so that even now, decades later, the simple act of walking down the sidewalk can sometimes trigger those feelings of fight, flight, or freeze. It's a stress response that comes up even though the laws of segregation are no longer in place, and few people today would even think of expecting her to move off the sidewalk. This is the kind of impact that lives on in our bodies after trauma of any kind, whether it be emotional trauma, marginalization, ridicule, or physical violence. These experiences live in our bodies.

Here is an example of a previous client, whom we will call "James." He was chronically insulted and ridiculed for not being like "the other boys" as a child and he experienced frequent bullying at school and at home for his burgeoning sexual orientation. Thus, he came to have a deeply unconscious core false belief that he was unlovable. On a conscious level, he yearned for love and connection. But his core false belief, the vibration he was expressing, worked against his yearning, and his experiences tended to reinforce that vibration. He repeatedly was attracted to, and fell for, men who could not possibly love him for various reasons. So, rather than providing James with the love that he sought, these relationships only reinforced his destructive core false belief.

James' story illustrates the power of unresolved trauma to perpetuate the original injury—in James' case the emotional trauma of his childhood was retriggered every time someone rejected him, in turn reinforcing the false belief in his own brokenness. When we resist the inner work of recognizing the impact of unresolved trauma on our life and our outlook, we aren't able to unlearn and undo the lies we've been told about ourselves. Until we do that deeper work, we will continue to replicate the relationships that confirm this negative core false belief. That's why we fall into unhealthy, even addictive patterns. That's why we say over and over again, "I thought he was going to be different" or "I thought this relationship was not going to be like the others." We simply can't find solutions to our inner turmoil by looking to the outer realm.

When we're in denial about what's authentically happening, our behaviors can become self-sabotaging. We've all seen it happen: people who appear to be incredibly focused and dedicated suddenly fail in a spectacular way. They do something to sabotage their own success. It's baffling because it seems out of character with what we see on the surface. But what's actually going on underneath is that the person is struggling with a core false belief about their own worthiness that stems from childhood trauma. Underneath all that striving, competition, and focus on success is an unconscious belief of "I'm not worthy." And this is the belief that trips them up in the crucial moment. So, trauma can block us from our full expression. Being in denial about what's really happening in the unconscious can prevent us from connecting spiritually with our true essence. The core false beliefs that result from unresolved trauma can trap us in a limited and limiting reality that keeps us from true healing.

Victim Consciousness

How does this relate to an addicted life? Remember, we're talking about addiction as a brilliant strategy that's no longer working; using something outside of ourselves to try to fix something that feels broken within. The connection is simple. If trauma has led us to walk around with a sense of brokenness, then we naturally turn to things outside ourselves to attempt to repair that feeling of brokenness. The trouble is, if we've allowed the trauma response to get buried in our subconscious, then it begins to run the show.

The trauma defines us and colors all our experiences. We come to believe that we are, fundamentally, victims. Let me be clear: This does not mean that we weren't possibly victimized when the trauma happened. I'm not saying that the trauma you underwent was your responsibility, or your fault. Not at all. What I am saying is that, because of the trauma, we can sometimes take on the *identity* of a victim. We can sometimes start believing and saying things like "I am a victim," or "I am powerless" which only concretizes this victim mentality into our consciousness.

Unfortunately, part of trauma's power is that it can lead us to believe that the brokenness it leaves us with is fundamental, it's an essential part of who we are. When we are victims of trauma we often fall into a sense of powerlessness or hopelessness, a belief that we are never going to be able to reconnect with the truth of who we are. This leaves us feeling like we're victims to the entire world. It leaves us feeling as if the problem is outside of us and so the solution must be outside of us as well. To me, that is addiction in its simplest form; trying to fix something that feels broken inside by turning to solutions on the outside.

Healing from Trauma

Healing when we've experienced trauma can involve all four rooms of our human house: the physical, emotional, mental, and spiritual. If you've suffered the ongoing effects of trauma, I invite you to start by working with a trauma specialist (for example, someone who specializes in Somatic Experiencing® or E.M.D.R.). This is someone who can help you to create safe places and relationships in which to break free from the cycle of replicating trauma in your life, and also begin to do the deeper inner work of unlearning: clearly looking within, recognizing the core false beliefs and the stories that you have about yourself and the world.

Then you can experience what I call "The Great Remembering," which is reconnecting with your essential self, waking up to this greater reality of who and what you are and from there witnessing life. In other words, when we unlearn and remember, we are no longer bound by our stories. We can break free from the traumatic stories that have trapped us in an old way of being and an old way of seeing the world that is at best limited but oftentimes replicates the trauma in ways that injure us at many levels. We will cover this in a more in-depth way in Section 2 of this book.

Chapter Two

SPIRITUAL DISCONNECTION

*The key problem I encounter working with wounded,
depressed, and unhappy people is a lack of connection...
starting from a disconnection from themselves and then
with others. This is why love often becomes so distorted
and destructive. When people experience a disconnection
from themselves, they feel it but do not realize the problem.*
— David W. Earle

What is Spiritual Disconnection?

"I am whole and perfect in every way." From a spiritual perspective,
life's journey can be seen as an attempt to reclaim this truth. In fact,
even our addictions can be a result of our attempts at restoration.
Even our addictions can come out of the attempt to restore the
connection to our true nature. Addictive behavior is categorically
a response to the felt sense that something is out of balance, that
we have forgotten our essential self, forgotten the truth of who and
what we are. In our addictive behavior, we are usually looking for
something outside of ourselves to help us manage something that
feels disturbed or broken within. It's a solution to the problem of
the fragmented self. In his book *The Four Agreements*, Don Miguel

Ruiz introduces us to the concept of "the domestication of the human"—the process whereby we receive messages about, in his words, *"who we should be, what we shouldn't be, who we (are), and who we (are) not."* That's what I'm talking about here as spiritual disconnection. It's the separation from our essential nature.

We come into this world as spiritual beings intuitively experiencing our oneness with Source. If you look at a very small child, you recognize this connection with the pristine self. My first book *Conscious Being* opens with the following story that illustrates this: A young couple had a toddler, and then they had a second baby. When they brought the baby home, they realized the toddler was tiptoeing and sneaking into the infant's room at night. Because they were curious about this, they put up a baby cam to record what the toddler was doing in the room. To their surprise they discovered that the toddler was leaning over the crib and saying to the infant, "Please tell me about God. I'm beginning to forget."

This is a powerful demonstration of the domestication of the human. We come into this world seeking the love that we know we are. We are designed to receive love, to see our love reflected back to us. But many of us don't experience that as small children. Or we do, but it's not enough. It's mixed up with other conflicting messages. From a very early age, life begins to teach us the opposite of what we come here intuitively knowing. We come into this world knowing our essential nature and our oneness with Source, but very quickly "the tall people" begin to teach us otherwise. These adults, often very loving and well-meaning, begin (quite often unconsciously) teaching us about "the world." They teach us attitudes and approaches to life like competition, fear, scarcity, and separation. I love the phrase "domestication of the human" because it calls to mind the domestication of wild animals. When we domesticate animals, we call it "breaking them," or "breaking their spirit." That's what happens to human beings as we enter this realm of existence. Most of us get taught all sorts of things that are a fundamental lie about who and what we genuinely are.

Attachment Theory

Attachment theory is a psychological model that endeavors to describe the dynamics of interpersonal relationships. The most important precept of attachment theory is that a baby needs to develop a loving relationship with at least one primary caregiver for the child's successful spiritual and emotional development, and for learning how to effectively normalize their emotions. In the presence of a sensitive and receptive caregiver, the infant will use the caregiver as a "safe base" from which to explore. This is not to say that anyone can parent "perfectly." For example, there are times when parents feel exhausted or preoccupied, or life distracts them with daily activities and tasks. So, even the most attentive parents can sever the attachment or connection. Because of these childhood experiences, as adults, we develop into one of these three different unhealthy attachment styles: avoidant, anxious, or anxious-avoidant. The intention is to move toward what is called secure attachment. I prefer to use the term authentic attachment.

The following are some characteristics of the four different attachment styles. Adults with avoidant attachment desire a high level of independence, often appearing to avoid attachment altogether. They view themselves as self-reliant, invulnerable to attachment feelings and not needing close relationships. They tend to suppress their feelings, dealing with rejection by distancing themselves from partners of whom they often have a poor opinion. Adults with anxious attachment seek elevated levels of intimacy, approval and receptiveness from partners, and can easily become overly dependent. They tend to be less trusting, have less positive views about themselves than the people in their lives, and may display high levels of emotional self-expression, worry and impulsiveness in their relationships. Adults with anxious-avoidant attachment have mixed feelings about close relationships, simultaneously desiring and feeling uncomfortable with emotional closeness. They tend to mistrust their partners and can often view themselves as unworthy. Similar to avoidant attached adults, anxious-avoidant adults tend to seek less intimacy, and suppress their feelings. Conversely, authentically attached adults foster positive views of themselves, their companions and their relationships. They feel comfortable with intimacy and independence, and have an easy time balancing the two.

We all want to experience connection. When we are disconnected from our essential self, we attempt to attach to something or someone in the external realm to find peace, happiness, or simply numb out the pain of feeling the deep disconnection. It is easy to see how the unhealthy external attachment styles can lead to many forms of addictions. In the most simplistic perspective, the pain of living with these detrimental attachment styles will "need" to be relieved in some way. And for anyone who has compulsive tendencies, this often provokes and fuels addictive behavior.

Core False Beliefs

If we're born with a solid connection to our divine nature, what happens to that connection? Most of us come into a world that teaches us about fear, separation, and competition. We learn things about ourselves and our world that are contrary to the fundamental truth that we are whole and perfect. Adults, often well-meaning, try to prepare us for the world by teaching us to fight, to wall off our emotions, to criticize. These lessons are based on lies that I call "core false beliefs." The deepest root of addiction is this: we learn and we appropriate core false beliefs, which break the connection with our true nature. This fragments us and pushes us to turn outward for validation, love, and peace of mind.

Let's look at an example: Sylvia's coworkers and acquaintances see her as an accomplished professional, a caring friend, and a loving mother. But her intimate relationships are crippled by a set of core false beliefs that sprang from a troubled childhood. They go something like this: "I am never going to succeed. Things are never going to go smoothly for me. I am never going to fix my life." Looking through the lens of these core false beliefs, Sylvia lives in a state of relentless disconnect between how she sees herself (failed, struggling, broken) and what she yearns for (success, ease, wholeness). So, no matter how much she accomplishes, she will never truly experience her own achievement. She gets extremely high marks on her annual evaluation at work, for instance, with only one small element tagged for improvement, yet she will never see this as success. Because of her core false beliefs, all she can focus on is that one area for improvement, which she interprets as a massive failure.

Just as Sylvia's core false beliefs trap her into seeing her life as a series of failures, they also trap her into a life of constant striving to achieve. Those false beliefs force Sylvia to hang onto the goal of success; striving for success becomes her addiction. Ashamed by her limitations, her mistakes, her perceived weakness, she's convinced that they are her true self. She pushes them into the shadow, hiding them from others as she tries to present a perfect image to the world. So, she works constantly at trying to be the perfect partner, the perfect employee, the perfect mother. Eventually, Sylvia turns to drugs and alcohol to find relief from the self-imposed pressure she is living with. Let me clarify one thing: The perfection Sylvia is after is not the perfection she was born into, it's not the wholeness that is her birthright. It's a distorted version of that original perfection. Sylvia tries to wrest it from outside herself instead of finding and connecting with what she essentially is.

Brilliant Strategies

Our core false beliefs, which frequently stem from generalized unresolved trauma and spiritual disconnection, may leave us feeling broken. In response, we might look for things to make that feeling go away. That is often the foundational malady of addictive behavior. I have seen it repeatedly: What is most often at the core of addictive behavior is this sense of brokenness within and the search for something outside ourselves to help us manage the resulting discomfort. Looked at in this way, addictive behavior can be seen as a strategy, even a brilliant strategy, for survival. When our sense of self is fragmented, when we see ourselves as fundamentally broken, that's a very, very painful way to live. We feel like we're surviving rather than thriving, walking around with a sense of separation, a feeling of fear, a belief that we can't reveal our true selves because there's something wrong with us. And when we discover something like gambling or sex or drugs, it can bring us relief from that terrible pain. Many clients have told me that their addiction was the most consistent relationship in their life. That's a powerful awareness.

Addictive behavior is a strategy that may work for a long time; it might succeed in protecting us from the desperation that might otherwise overwhelm us. If Sylvia suddenly lost her work or her family, for instance, then she might be overwhelmed by the sense of worthlessness that fuels her workaholism, and it might prove too much for her to bear. Her addiction to accomplishment keeps her alive, at least for now. I, myself used drugs and alcohol to numb the pain of my core false beliefs; my substance abuse kept me from killing myself or losing my sanity. For me, drugs and alcohol were a brilliant strategy that worked well—until they stopped serving me.

It's not just a matter of basic survival or avoiding suicide or insanity. Our addictive strategies can help us make sense of the world and find relief from pain and suffering. If we have a core belief that the world is not safe—if that is our lived experience, our reality—then we tend to develop strategies for making these beliefs more bearable. We might shut down emotionally, refusing to open to others. We might implement stringent physical security measures to try to protect ourselves and our families. We might become overly controlling. These things serve not only to keep us from spiraling into a state of chronic anxiety but also to validate our core false belief in the inherent danger of life.

Addiction is a Brilliant Strategy

We often hear addictive behavior described in other terms—as a disease, or as a coping mechanism. Both can seem inherently negative in connotation. They suggest that there's something wrong that needs to be fixed. "I am an addict and that's what's wrong." In the western medical model, the problem is the disease of addiction, and it's addressed by treating the symptoms, whether they be physical, social, or emotional. And calling addiction a "coping mechanism" suggests that a person is less able to function than "normal" people and needs the crutch of the addictive behavior to get along in life.

Both perspectives have their place in our recovery. But they are limited. They both see addiction as the problem rather than as a sign that something is out of alignment internally, on the spiritual level. They are based on a negative assessment of addictive behavior ("it's the problem"), and this makes it difficult to see anything else. Reframing addiction as a brilliant strategy, as a self-preserving human response to a problem, removes the negative judgment from our perspective and invites us to ask ourselves a couple of key questions: "What is my addictive behavior a response to? What problem is it trying to solve?" As a brilliant strategy, addictive behavior—whether it using drugs and alcohol, gambling, sex, work, etc.—can serve to bring relief from a profound sense of uneasiness in the world, of disconnection and fragmentation. Recognizing addictive behavior as a brilliant strategy gives us clarity about what's authentically happening inside. It tells us something about the wholeness we are truly seeking. It tells us, with terrifying clarity, where we're stuck, where we're shut down, and where we're closed off. Then we can simply ask the questions: "Is this strategy still working? Is it still serving me? Is there a better way?"

Other Brilliant Strategies

Using a substance like alcohol or drugs is only one of the brilliant strategies people use to deal with the pain of spiritual disconnection. There are many, many others. If we suffer, like Sylvia, from the core false belief that we are fundamentally broken, then we might keep the pain of that belief at bay with the brilliant strategy of maintaining "good" behavior; following the rules and striving for success. If we see the world as chaotic, then we might numb the resulting fear by keeping our lives as ordered and tidy as possible. If we believe that we lack the inner strength or virtue to truly belong anywhere, then we might try to make things "right" by surrendering ourselves to some external power "out there," like God, a program, or a group.

One thing to be aware of is noticing if new "strategies" or addictions start to emerge once you let go of your primary addiction. This is often called "cross-addiction" because new addictions can surface as we move away from the original substance or behavior. I've heard it referred to as "whack-a-mole" because new addictions can pop up as we move into recovery. Remaining aware of this and practicing the tools and principles introduced in this book can assist you in deepening your recovery rather than switching to new addictions.

The Inward Journey

Whichever brilliant strategies we practice, they are most likely directed outward because we're seeing the solution as external. It seems like most addictions come out of a victim's perspective, in which we see life as something that happens *to* us. Our problems are caused by other people, by institutions like school or government, even by God—everything is caused by circumstances beyond our control, forces we can't manage. Often this viewpoint stems from our earliest experiences, which taught us that we are powerless to change anything directly and that the only way to get something we need is by sheer force or manipulation. Victim consciousness leaves us feeling powerless over circumstances, and other people's behavior seems to have way too much impact on our lives. This viewpoint offers us little choice. We feel trapped.

Living this way is excruciatingly painful so, of course, we're going to look outside ourselves for something to numb that pain. Our happiness depends on other people and external circumstances, so we try to manipulate those things to get what we want: "If I could just make enough money ... If my boss would just recognize me ..." or "Everything will be fine if I acknowledge that I am a total failure and rely on God."

Whatever our brilliant strategy, chances are it will initially work, sometimes even for years. If it doesn't, we'll find a different strategy. But ultimately, all outward-directed strategies end up affirming that there's something wrong with us and that something out there is going to fix us. These strategies limit our responses to life. If things do not go the way we want, we can only conclude that it's because we have done something wrong, or because we *are* wrong. Ultimately, our brilliant strategies stop working because they are limited. They are inadequate in that they bring only temporary relief from feelings of fragmentation. And they are limiting in that they ultimately strengthen and solidify our belief in our own powerlessness; they offer no other perspective.

Seeing addictive behavior as a brilliant strategy for minimizing pain and staying alive helps us to ask the further questions, "Is my addiction still working as a solution? Is the strategy still brilliant?" Maybe for you it is. Maybe for now there's too much going on in your life and you need to keep seeing the world as you've always seen it. Maybe you're not ready or able at this time to look any deeper. However, I want to encourage you to investigate a little further here. Why did you pick up this book? Has something happened in your life that caused you to question whether there might be another way? Are you tired of trying to orchestrate everything around you to maintain stability? Could it be that you're ready to sit with the discomfort of this healing work if that means finding a deeper recovery?

Our spiritual development isn't always linear. When we're challenged by something that triggers an old pattern, we might slip from a new understanding back into an earlier one. One moment we might be feeling full of confidence and trust that everything is working out, and the next moment we are back in a feeling of powerlessness. So, it might serve us to be patient with ourselves and open to what the process is wanting to reveal to us.

My invitation to you in this moment is to really go within and ask yourself: "What is the main strategy that I have been using to try to feel more whole and more connected, or to feel less pain? And is that strategy still working?" If not, are you ready to make a conscious choice to move on? Are you ready to start recognizing that you have been making choices all along? Your addiction was a choice, a brilliant strategy to keep you safe, or whole, or alive. It may be time to let it go and see what else is out there. And, more accurately, see what else is inside of you.

Shifting Consciousness

When the strategy of your addiction is no longer working, when your addictive behaviors have become maladaptive and no longer function to bring you a sense of relief, then they become what we might call a dis-ease. Or rather, they become a side-effect, as it were, of your underlying spiritual disconnection. Not only do your addictive behaviors stop working, they begin to cause more problems, more separation. So, the very thing you've been using to try to get more connection, or at least to relieve your sense of disconnection, is now causing more separation. Now you've got a different problem on your hands, one that requires a new solution, a new way of living. When the strategy of your addiction is failing so acutely that you are desperate, you may just become willing to step out of the path you know and try a different way. That's when you can experience a shift in consciousness.

Let's take alcohol for example, because it's a very common addiction. Drinking is a solution that works well in the beginning but eventually causes separation rather than connection. When alcohol goes from being a brilliant solution to being the focus of our lives, it can cause damage to our relationships, our ability to function in the workplace, and so on. We're all familiar with what happens when the brilliant strategy of using alcohol stops working.

Let's say you have entered recovery because of the ill effects of your addiction, but you haven't looked at the causes of the addictive behavior. You might think, "I'm solving the problem of my addiction, so now I will feel better!" But when you put down the alcohol, when you let go of that addiction, what may very well happen instead is that you now start to feel the pain of the unresolved trauma, spiritual disconnection, or toxic shame that caused the addiction in the first place. Even after you've recovered physically, you might still feel awful. That's because you've let go of the solution, not the problem. Yes, you needed to let it go. But it was a solution that played a very key role in your life, perhaps for many, many years. Recognizing this as a loss opens a doorway to some of the inner work that will bring deeper healing.

A New Way of Being

How we perceive the world is how we experience the world. When we change our perspective, the world seems to change. But this may not always be easy. Letting go of a strategy that you've been using for a long time is not always a straightforward process. So, as you work through this book you'll be learning not only what's at the root of your addiction, but more importantly, how to use spiritual practices to move forward into a new way of being. It's one that can help you return to a sense of wholeness and peace. These disciplines include tools for nurturing your ability to be truly present and conscious, like meditation and an awareness of language. We'll also look at the importance of creating a safe place, building community, and developing authenticity. All along we'll be doing the work of uncovering and dismantling those strategies that no longer serve you and the ideas and beliefs that lie beneath them.

Perhaps you've walked around for years, maybe for as long as you can remember, with beliefs about who and what you are that leave you feeling broken and shattered. Maybe you are beginning to see that these beliefs have caused you to bury whole portions of yourself into the shadow, never to be shared with others. Perhaps you recognize that much of what you do feels out of your control because this strategy is no longer working for you, it's now trapping you. If so, you're in a place of shifting consciousness. It can be a daunting place, because you're letting go of the tried and true and are waiting for something new, something you can't see yet. Let me reassure you: You can get through this. Beyond this seemingly fragmented self lies your essential self, which has always been there, whole and perfect, unharmed and unharmable. I want to reiterate that, underneath all the addictive behavior, you are whole and perfect in every way, right in this moment. And my invitation for you is to tap deeply into that truth and see what happens.

Chapter Three

TOXIC SHAME

The first element of shame resilience is recognizing shame and understanding our triggers. Men and women who are resilient to shame have this capacity. This enables them to respond to shame with awareness and understanding. When we can't recognize shame and understand our triggers, shame blindsides us. It washes over us, and we want to slink away and hide. In contrast, if we recognize our shame triggers, we can make mindful, thoughtful decisions about how we're going to respond to shame—before we do something that might make things worse. Shame has physical symptoms. These might include your mouth getting dry, time seeming to slow down, your heart racing, twitching, looking down and tunnel vision. These symptoms are different from one person to the next. So if you learn your physical symptoms, you can recognize shame and get back on your feet faster.

— *Brené Brown*

What Is Toxic Shame?

As we've seen, a spiritual perspective provides us with a broad view of addiction and recovery. Many of us, even if we're in recovery or are not actively addicted to a substance like alcohol or drugs, experience an addiction to outer circumstances, to an outer-focused life. Therefore, it is important to adopt a spiritual approach to our healing, along with physical, mental, and emotional perspectives. A spiritual approach helps us identify what lies at the root of our addiction.

Taking this spiritual perspective, we see that for people who struggle long-term with an addiction, the root causes are three-fold: unresolved trauma, spiritual disconnection, and toxic shame. We looked at unresolved trauma in chapter 1, and disconnection and fragmentation in chapter 2. In this chapter, we're going to be talking about toxic shame and how a shame-based experience and a shame-based life can lead to addiction in all its various forms. We'll look at the distinction between shame and guilt, and we'll also consider the importance of language in framing our reality.

In his book *Healing the Shame That Binds You*, John Bradshaw writes: "*Toxically shamed people tend to become more and more stagnant as life goes on. They live in a guarded, secretive, and defensive way. They try to be more than human—perfect and controlling—or less than human—losing interest in or stagnated in some addictive behavior.*" Does this sound familiar?

What is toxic shame? How can we recognize it in ourselves? Quite simply, shame is a sense of brokenness, a sense that "something is deeply, fundamentally, inherently wrong with me." Brené Brown, as many of you know, is an incredible writer and researcher who studies vulnerability and shame. In one of her TED Talks, she describes shame in this way: "*Shame drives two big tapes: 'Never good enough,' and if you can talk it out of that one, 'Who do you think you are?'*"

Guilt vs. Shame

One way to think about shame is to compare it with guilt. With guilt, we believe we have *done* something wrong, or something that we believe is wrong. With guilt, we can say, "I'm sorry—I made a mistake." With shame, however, there's a belief that we *are* a mistake, we *are* wrong. The way we work with guilt is very different than the way we work with shame, because when we are coming from a place of guilt—meaning that we have done something that we feel is wrong—we can try to remedy the situation in one way or another. Guilt is generally about a behavior, and it gets fixed behaviorally. Shame is something deeper, more rooted in who we believe we are. And relinquishing it requires deeper, more internal work.

It's easy to confuse guilt with shame. As part of your recovery program, you might go out and make amends to someone but then feel worse afterward, because in taking a behavioral approach you are only clearing up the guilt, but might not address the underlying shame. The potential of this process is it may actually produce more shame and you could even be re-traumatizing yourself, because it could bring up these deeper feelings that you have not worked through yet. If you haven't done the work on shame that's needed, and if you haven't addressed the core false belief that you are wrong, it won't be enough to work on your guilt. Of course, making amends is a powerful, spiritual practice that can bring wonderful results, but it's also important to be aware of the possibility that there is underlying shame which will need to be addressed as well.

If your core belief is "I'm not lovable," then it's only natural to think something like, "If only this person would accept my amends, then I'd be OK," or "If only I could convince her I'm worthy, then everything would be fine." But if you believe this, if you believe the amends process will eradicate your shame, you might be disappointed. Simply put, shame doesn't get resolved that way. The key here is to make the amends for the sake of making the amends, rather than hoping *you* feel better in doing so.

Working with Shame

Continuing with the case study from an earlier chapter: As part of his recovery, James started to make amends. One of the first people he wanted to make amends to was his father. When they met, James apologized: "I'm sorry for all the things I have done wrong." His father didn't say much at the time, but later James got a letter from him that said, "Thank you so much; it's great to have my son back." Effective amends, right? Not necessarily. Somehow, for James, the amends didn't bring the relief he was hoping for and he was left feeling confused and hurt. Although he knew he was supposed to focus on his "side of the street," he couldn't help but wish that his father had made amends, too. Because of this expectation, and because of the underlying toxic shame, he felt re-wounded, and then he judged himself for feeling that way. What James didn't understand is that much of his deeply rooted shame arose from the relationship with his father. He had possibly made amends too early, before he had resolved his toxic shame. It's not that making amends was the "wrong" thing to do; it did move James along in his process. It simply wasn't enough.

Another important point to address is this: Many times we will hear people say, "I feel so ashamed that I did that." The idea here is that we feel shame because of our behavior. I actually want to introduce a different possibility. What if the shame actually drives the behavior, rather than the other way around? In my experience, when we are holding a deep sense of shame about ourselves, our behavior comes as a result of that shame. Simply said, "hurt" people "hurt" people. And then the "shameful" behavior brings on even *more* shame. This is what we refer to as a shame spiral.

Sources of Toxic Shame

Most people experience some shame, but some of us have toxic shame. Shame becomes toxic over time as we continue to believe we are damaged and broken. Some of us believe deeply that there is something essentially wrong with us—that is, there's no way to fix the brokenness because it's part of who we are. And the greater the toxic shame, the greater its correlation with addiction. How does this happen? Remember the four rooms of the self as described in the introduction—physical, mental, emotional, and spiritual? Well, simply stated, when we hear repeated negative messages in any of these aspects of self, we can pick up and internalize them as core beliefs about ourselves, beliefs that are not true, at least not the ultimate truth of who we are.

Toxic shame, for the most part, gets created quite early in life, often in a broken family system where there is a repeated message that we are not good enough or there's something wrong with us. This sort of message comes to many children early in life, but not all of them develop toxic shame. It's when we hear a repeated message that there is something wrong with us, when we receive this message repeatedly in the physical, mental, emotional, and/or spiritual realm, that we begin to take on an *identity* of brokenness. It may also be that certain people are more sensitive to identity-building messages than others. Whatever the case, if we develop toxic shame then eventually we don't even need to hear those messages anymore because we have become so adept at repeating them to ourselves. We have internalized the negative voices and have become perpetuators of our own toxic shame.

Another Brené Brown insight is instructive here: "*Three things allow toxic shame to thrive and become the way we see ourselves: secrecy, silence, and judgment.*" Often people with toxic shame come from families that carry a big secret, about which everyone is silent. If a family's secret has nurtured a toxic sense of shame, then the last thing anyone will want to do is bring that secret into the light. So there we have secrecy and silence. Thirdly, there's judgment. Toxic shame thrives in an environment where people are not seen for who they are, perfect and worthy of love, but are constantly judged for who they are *not*, for standards that they fail to meet. If we live in an atmosphere of judgment, then the need for silence and secrecy only becomes greater, because we will never feel safe enough to present or even comprehend our authentic selves.

The Impact of Toxic Shame

So, what does toxic shame do to us? Why is it such a destructive thing? First, there's a physical consequence. Our perspective on life and the feeling tone we are holding about ourselves affect our health in many ways. Our core beliefs affect not only the way we see ourselves and the world, but also affect our central nervous system. There's a correlation between toxic shame and real diagnosable illness: not only addiction, but depression, anxiety syndromes, eating disorders, and the like. When a person has an identity of brokenness, it can create illness not only in their emotional and spiritual lives, but in their physical lives as well. Toxic shame can lead to literal cancer and disease in all forms. Another result of toxic shame, and of the secrecy, silence, and judgment that allow it to thrive, is that it drives people to try to fix or hide their essential brokenness with all sorts of unhealthy behaviors. When there is a sense of brokenness internally, we often look incessantly for something outside ourselves to assuage the pain of that brokenness or to at least make sure no one else can see it.

Thus, if a person has an unhealthy sense of self and their core false belief is "I'm not lovable," then he or she may very well become obsessed with finding an impeccable relationship. If the core false belief is "I'm not good enough," then the person may become an overachiever. If your core false belief is "I'm not safe," then you may always be searching for stability and security. You may spend your whole life building walls, literal and figurative, in an attempt to feel safer. This external search for solutions doesn't have to be conscious; as a matter of fact, it's usually unconscious. But it's there, an unending, insatiable need that you can't stop trying to satisfy even though you'll never be able to, at least not from the outside.

Another consequence of toxic shame is that it's contagious. It gets projected outward. So, when we believe that there's something wrong with who and what we are, we're going to project that out into the world. We're going to begin to experience the world as broken simply because that's what we believe about ourselves. People with toxic shame begin to see that brokenness everywhere in their external reality for the simple reason that people tend to see what they expect to see. We unconsciously long for the brokenness in other people and situations.

The Importance of Language

This tendency to see what you expect to see, to project your core beliefs outward, is very powerfully manifest in what you say, in your words. So, if you're walking around believing, "I am a mess" or "I am a loser," or "I am unattractive," then chances are you will also say these things, in one way or another. And the very act of verbalizing this false belief reinforces those fundamental lies about who and what you are. And of course, from there, the tendency is to seek relief in all types of unhealthy external behaviors. Therefore, it's important to recognize the power of language, specifically the power of the "I am." What you attach your "I am" to is quite powerful. Every time you say (or think), "I am _____ (a drunk, boring, stupid, etc.)," you reinforce a lie about yourself. In my counseling work, when I can help someone move from "I am" to "I have," there is often a powerful shift.

For example, some years ago my friend Gavin told me that he had been saying "I am depressed" for a long time and had recently come to realize what he was saying. Once he noticed this, he also realized that the more he continued to believe and express the belief, "I am depressed," the more depressed he felt. But when he shifted to saying "I have depression" or "I feel depressed," everything began to change. He was able draw the important distinction between being depressed and having the experience of depression. Saying "I have depression" allowed him to start to see the depression as something nonessential and changeable, rather than as something fundamental to his identity. This opened him up to his essential self, his true self, which wasn't depressed. This true self was beyond the symptoms of depression.

Gavin's story had a profound impact on me and dramatically shifted the way I work. I started to work on helping people shift from statements like: "I am an addict," "I am broken," "I am damaged in some way," to "I have these things about myself that want to be healed." A profound healing realization can happen when we make that shift because for the first time we have identified the truth of who and what we are not as brokenness, but as something else, something more positive and powerful. In other words, when we can finally shine some light on our inner dialogue and witness that these seemingly broken portions of ourselves are not essential, but are changeable, then we can start to open to the possibility that our true self is something much more profoundly beautiful and whole.

My invitation to you today is to take a moment and really ask yourself, "How am I speaking to myself? What am I attaching my 'I am' to?" My hope is that it will be possible to shift that language to something that's more accurate, and that the distinction that this creates will make further room for what you genuinely are: "I am whole and perfect; I am love; I am lovable." We'll look at this process further in chapter 5, "Unlearning." For now, just imagine what might happen if you were to shift this focus from something that seems broken about yourself into something that supports your wholeness and healing.

Pain and Suffering

Pain seems to be a part of the human experience. Naturally, most of us prefer to feel loved, safe, and connected rather than sad, lonely, or afraid. But the latter feelings seem to be a part of life. In Buddhism, the First Noble Truth states that: *"Pain in life is inevitable but suffering is not. Pain is what the world does to you, suffering is what you do to yourself. Pain is inevitable, suffering is optional."* Suffering is optional because it is the result of how we deal with or process the experience of pain. Pain and pleasure are in the body. Suffering is in the mind. One root cause of suffering is resisting pain and attaching to pleasure. Another is clinging to the idea that things in the external world need to look or be a certain way.

Pain is an internal navigational system, informing us that something needs our attention. If we resist or ignore the sounding of pain's guidance, we prolong it and create unnecessary suffering. In fact, when we resist anything that is happening in our internal *or* external experience, we create unnecessary suffering. When we refuse to let go of what no longer serves a purpose in our lives, clinging to what once was, we also create unnecessary suffering.

Suffering ceases when we bring ourselves into full alignment with what is, trusting the unfolding of life moment to moment. Suffering ceases when we stop resisting inevitable outer change. For, no matter what happens, we possess the creative power within us to pick ourselves up and continue in the direction of our heart's desires. Suffering ceases when we are willing to fully accept the whole gamut of our emotions, without judgment. For when we allow ourselves to fully feel what we feel, we understand that emotions exist as a wave of energy moving through us, and are temporary. Suffering ceases when we are willing to release what no longer serves us, even though it previously had purpose in our lives, knowing that life will bring us what we need, when we need it.

Activating Empathy

Another incredible tool for allowing us to open and move beyond shame is empathy. Empathy is one antidote to the corrosive impact of shame. For shame lives in the shadow, it thrives on secrecy and judgment in a world where we believe that we are broken but that everyone else is fine. Shame says, "If I let you see the real me, you will laugh at me, leave me, hurt me, etc." But empathy breaks through these falsehoods. Empathy shows us that we live in a community of people with similar experiences. To be empathetic, to say, "Yes, I honor your feelings. I have also had that struggle," requires the courage to be genuine and to let others see what's actually happening with us. And the amazing thing is that people respond to this.

Empathy and authenticity are closely linked. Authenticity is powerful because it's expansive—when you're able to be authentic, others tend to relate to that and, in turn, they let you see them. The truth ends up being the opposite of our core false belief: it's not "If I let you see the real me, you will leave," but "If I let you see the real me, you will often let me see the real you." Before you can reveal your authentic self, you first need to feel safe in your own skin. So, my invitation to you is this: If you are walking around with a sense of brokenness, if you are walking around with a sense that there is something essentially wrong with you, I want to encourage you right now to think about what safety might look or feel like to you. We'll work on this more in chapter 4, "Creating Safety," but for now just start to play with the possibility that there's a safe place for you that will help you show the world your real self.

Bringing Shame into the Light

In this chapter, we've looked at one of the roots of addiction: toxic shame. As we have seen, toxic shame comes out of core false beliefs about ourselves, nurtured in silence, secrecy, and judgment. Initially these beliefs may have functioned to protect us or to make sense of the world, but at some point, they stopped working, leading only to this crippling belief in our fundamental brokenness. We can start moving away from toxic shame by being conscious of our self-definitions, by looking for ways to shift them to the positive, and by creating safe places from which to nurture our true, authentic selves.

For me, the spiritual journey to recovery is not about learning— it's about unlearning. Unlearning all those false beliefs and ideas that we've collected about ourselves and the world. On the spiritual journey, we come to recognize that subconscious thoughts do not *have* to run the show. We recognize that we can bring our false beliefs into conscious awareness, and we can work with shame by nurturing a safe space in which to bring it out of the shadow. This is not a journey that starts, or ends, when we get sober. It starts years earlier, before we accepted any of these false beliefs, back when we were young children, filled with wonder. You were once a whole and perfect child. And to reclaim the truths that you were born with, to genuinely see yourself as whole and perfect, it will help to practice looking within at what your core false beliefs are.

I know with my whole being that you can break free of this. Understanding the three roots of addiction, unresolved trauma, spiritual disconnection, and toxic shame, is the first step in restoring your true knowledge—that you are fundamentally whole and perfect and one with Spirit. You've come a long way. Now, in Part 2, I invite you to explore how to break the cycle of addiction through the steps we've outlined here: creating safety, unlearning, and practicing spiritual principles.

PART 2

BREAKING THE CYCLE
OF ADDICTION

In Part 1 of this book, we looked at the roots of
addiction: unresolved trauma, spiritual disconnection,
and toxic shame. In the next three chapters, we're going
to explore how to break the cycle of addiction which
results from our loss of connection, from the core false
beliefs borne of trauma that created toxic shame.

Chapter 4 will focus on inner and outer safety:
why this inner work requires a space of safety and
ways we can create those spaces. It also addresses
the importance of self-love and acceptance.

Chapter 5 will delve deeper into the process of
unlearning: uncovering our core false beliefs to
see what lies beneath them in order to live more
deeply in the truth of who and what we are.

Chapter 6 will introduce some spiritual principles and
practices that can help us break the cycle of addiction
and the limited and limiting ways we see the world.

Chapter Four

CREATING SAFETY

My coming to faith did not start with a leap but rather a series of staggers from what seemed like one safe place to another. Like lily pads, round and green, these places summoned and then held me up while I grew. Each prepared me for the next leaf on which I would land, and in this way I moved across the swamp of doubt and fear.

— *Anne Lamott*

To break free from the cycle of addiction we need to connect with and recognize the truth of who and what we are. This process involves a deep look inward, as we lovingly identify and unlearn the core false beliefs that are keeping us from seeing ourselves as whole and perfect. Looking inward and letting go can be daunting, especially if part of our strategy for survival has been to freeze our inner life. So, we start by creating safety, developing a safe space from which to do this deeper work of inner clearing. Creating safety means opening our hearts, practicing self-love and acceptance, rebuilding trust, creating and honoring community, and nurturing conscious awareness. It may not seem easy to shift our perspectives in this way, but it's incredibly rewarding. When we can create a strong foundation of safety, our inner work and spiritual practices take on transformative meaning and power. That's why creating safety is the important first step in *Conscious Recovery*.

Creating External Safety

Before we explore methods to begin breaking the cycle of addictive and destructive behavior, I want to make clear the importance of external safety. In essence, external safety means being safe from physical, mental, emotional, and spiritual harm, and creating an encouraging network of support. External safety is the first priority. It is wise to ensure our basic physical safety, for example, before undertaking the deeper work that this chapter describes. This might involve changing our living situation to be free of an unhealthy relationship, or to not be surrounded by people who could be detrimental to our recovery, like someone who is active in an addiction. One example of this is that many people choose to live in a sober living environment in early recovery.

We can look at *external* safety from the perspective of each of the four rooms—physical, mental, emotional, and spiritual. In the physical room is the relationship with your body and its interaction with the physical world. In this room, recovery involves creating external safety from any kind of instability. The mental room houses your thoughts and ideas, the assumptions and expectations that shape your perspective on the world. Recovery in this room involves creating a safe space to examine your inner dialogue, the ways you describe yourself and the world. This may be a treatment program, a trusted counselor, or another type of support group. Recovery in the emotional room, the seat of feeling, and in the spiritual room, where we connect with our innermost self and with the Source that lies within all reality, requires a more internal process of creating safety, but also often requires an external structure as well, such as a supportive community, which will be discussed in more detail later in this chapter.

The rest of this chapter will focus primarily on *internal* safety. The discussion of safety here assumes that your external situation is stable and that you're externally safe. If you're not safe externally—if you're in a violent relationship, if you are feeling suicidal, if you're struggling with stable housing, if you're in any way threatened—please focus on your overall external well-being first. It is important to feel supported and stable enough to explore the inner work that recovery requires. As a matter of fact, I do not recommend you proceed through the rest of this book until you have a degree of external safety.

Maintaining an Open Heart

In the preface of this book I described a pivotal experience from my childhood: at the dinner table one night, when I felt myself physically closing off, shutting down, and building walls around my heart. This was my survival instinct kicking in—I shut down to protect myself from a seemingly threatening world that felt like it was becoming too dangerous. You might recall a similar experience in your own life. As I stated previously, this closing off was a brilliant strategy at the time because it literally saved my life. But living with a closed heart is not an effective long-term solution. I closed my heart off to protect myself, but that also closed me off from experiencing love and connection, which is what we all seem to desire. So, even as I was yearning to connect, I was closing myself *off* from connection. I was unconsciously choosing the so-called security of isolation over the deeper safety of joy, love and connection.

Living for long with a closed heart is painful and exhausting— because we're not built to thrive in isolation, we're not designed to live in the world cut off from love and connection. For me, life became so painful that I tried to ease my suffering through alcohol and drugs. They worked for a while, but eventually stopped serving their purpose and became addictive. What I needed then was to unlearn the strategies that were no longer working so I could open my heart, once again. There's a paradox here. We try to make ourselves secure by closing ourselves off, putting up walls and barriers, hiding our pain and even our essential selves in the shadow. While that may work at first, ultimately this strategy doesn't make us safe. It reaches its limits, leaving us feeling cut-off and alone. So, the first step toward true safety is recognizing how we have shut down. Then we can make a conscious choice to begin to open up.

For many of us, the shutting down is not a conscious choice. Instead, it's a deeply unconscious reaction to what we're experiencing about ourselves and our world. When I had that experience of closing off at age seven, I didn't consciously know what had just happened in my life. My feeling tone was one of brokenness, in other words, I was holding the energy of shame. I did make the decision to shut down, but I did so unconsciously, without understanding what I was undertaking or what the consequences would be. So, when I got into recovery and came into metaphysical teachings, it was important for me to recognize that, on an unconscious level, I had made this decision to close off, to shut down and keep people away, to create what I thought was safety.

Creating Internal Safety

As my experience illustrates, we've got it backwards when we think we need to keep people at an emotional distance to have safety. True safety gets created not by closing ourselves off, but by opening our hearts, and being willing to connect with compassionate people who support our recovery. This can possibly be challenging if we have a deeply held unconscious strategy of keeping people at a distance. This "distance keeping" may help us to *feel* safe, but is it really working? Moving from an unconscious closing off to a conscious opening of our hearts is an important step. It's an ongoing experience—moment by moment we make the decision to maintain our inner vulnerability, to open up and experience everything we're uncovering. Buddhist teacher and author, Pema Chödrön, states this so beautifully: "*The only reason we don't open our hearts and minds to other people is that they trigger confusion in us that we don't feel brave enough or sane enough to deal with. To the degree that we look clearly and compassionately at ourselves, we feel confident and fearless about looking into someone else's eyes.*"

That process looks different for everyone. It may come through counseling; it may come through being a part of a spiritual community. In whatever way you accomplish this, my invitation for you is to look within and ask these questions: "Am I open? Am I receptive? Is my heart open to this connection? Am I open to this miraculous way of being that is all around me, and certainly within me?"

Developing Self-Love

To unlearn our core false beliefs, to look inward at what is keeping us locked in unhealthy patterns, we need to create safe spaces for ourselves, correct? But this can be problematic for many of us who are struggling with addiction, in part because of the way we perceive ourselves and reality. We might habitually view ourselves in terms of "right" and "wrong;" perhaps we think recovery is about fixing ourselves. But this judging approach does little to help us create safety. People don't often feel safe when they are judged; they feel safe when they are loved and accepted. Deep inner change comes not from identifying what needs to be fixed, but from identifying what's in the way of our natural experience of the love we are. The Sufi poet Rumi states it this way: *"Your task is not to seek for love, but merely to seek and find all the barriers within yourself that you have built against it."*

Many of us believe our addiction is the problem. We don't like how addiction makes us feel or behave, so we think that once we let go of the addiction, the problem will be solved. We break the addictive habit because we think the addiction is wrong. When we start looking around, we can see that much of the way the world has been structured is based on this approach: identifying the problem and removing or solving it. We can see this approach in the work place. We see it in the educational system and in government, we see it in the western medical model, which asks, "What's the symptom? How do we get rid of it?" And of course, we see it in recovery models that, in effect, identify the addiction as the problem, and the addict as "wrong."

This perspective—that the addiction is the problem—has broader implications as well. When we treat addiction as the problem, what we're ultimately doing is supporting a worldview that says the way to grow and improve is to say, "What's wrong here?" and then fix it. This means that if we want to recover, then we need to be self-critical. "If we can just identify what's wrong, if we can just fix certain things about ourselves, then we can change." Again, this defines the person who has an addiction as broken in some way. Does this perspective work in the long run? It may work for a while, and of course at certain points in our recovery we do need to identify things we want to change. However, if we maintain this perspective long-term, we will quite possibly continue to unconsciously create more brokenness in our lives.

Overcoming Self-Criticism

Often when we remove the addictive behavior, what is left is the pain and disconnection that brought about the behavior in the first place.

And eventually, looking at addiction as something wrong or looking at the person who is in an addiction as broken in some way will only concretize the core false beliefs that underlie the addiction. Self-criticism is limited. It can deteriorate our self-worth and efficacy. If we're looking primarily through the lens of self-criticism rather than the lens of self-love, we can get stuck in a repetitive cycle of addiction. Habitual self-judgment reinforces one's belief in a broken self.

The spiritual perspective allows us to recognize that our addictive behavior, whatever it is, has been a solution, a strategy for addressing something that feels damaged within. The addictive behavior masks or soothes deep pain and a sense of disconnection that results from the core false beliefs we hold. Looking at it this way allows us to see ourselves, or any person with an addiction, with love and acceptance, and as someone who is in pain and needs connection. This takes courage. It also requires us to turn off our judgment—that habit of looking at ourselves and others, at situations and circumstances, in terms of "right" and "wrong." When we can let go of our judgment, we are open to a profound self-love and acceptance that is more than merely "being good to yourself." This self-love and acceptance means accepting yourself fully, even all your past behaviors. It means shifting your perspective, your habitual way of seeing yourself and the world. In the end, it becomes profoundly simple; which is a more effective way to open up to change, love or judgment?

Embracing Self-Acceptance

It can be difficult to shift our focus because the addictive behavior can appear so deeply "wrong" and our cultural mindset of looking to identify and solve the problem is so prevalent. So, let me reiterate: I'm not saying that letting go of judgment means we aren't accountable for behaviors we want to let go of. Many of us have broken trust with others, and with ourselves, and there are things we need to do to heal that broken trust. Letting go of judgment allows us to ask the questions, "What am I really looking for? and "Are there healthier ways to seek it?"

Early in my recovery I heard someone say, "Recovery is not about changing yourself—it's about loving and accepting yourself." At the time this made no sense because all I could see was how much was wrong in my life and how much I needed to change. What I couldn't see at the time is this: Love and acceptance are much more powerful change agents than judgment. Miraculous things can happen when I shift my approach from changing this or that about myself—from "What's wrong here? What needs to be fixed?"—to radical self-love and acceptance, or "What's right here? What can be celebrated?"

This approach focuses on what the addiction is authentically about, what it tells us. If we add to this the spiritual perspective, we receive even more. Recovery from the room of Spirit can help us see that what we're genuinely seeking is love and connection, which are found when we turn inward, to our essential nature. Spiritual recovery encourages us to be fully present, no matter how uncomfortable it may be. It gives us the safety we need to be in the moment and feel whatever it is we're truly feeling. Looking at what is truly being sought in the addictive behavior can be a powerful tool for us as we begin to unravel how our search for love and connection has been derailed and moved to the external realm by our core false beliefs about ourselves and the world. So, we shift from an outer-focused life to an inner-focused way of being and seeing. Again, it's a shift in focus.

Rebuilding Trust

This process can help build trust that has been damaged. When we break trust with someone, we need not only apologize, but we also need to change our behavior and begin to *become* trustworthy. And being trustworthy means being able to say what we mean and mean what we say. It means our actions start aligning with our intentions. Perhaps that's the greatest definition of trust: The sense of ourselves, who we are, is in alignment with what we say and do.

It's more difficult to create this alignment when we focus on fixing what's "wrong," because that focus doesn't encourage us to totally trust *ourselves*. When we are working from a perspective of self-judgment and criticism, it is the opposite of trust. But, when we perceive ourselves and others through the lens of love and acceptance and focus on what's working and what's truly behind our addiction, we start to reveal who we authentically are. When we see what's fueling our addictive behavior, our motivations become clearer. When we become aware of our self-talk, our inner dialogue, we can take responsibility for it. And that's a more solid foundation for building authentic trust. We can then be well on our way to rebuilding trust with ourselves and others.

It may take time to rebuild trust with the people in your life. Remember, you have probably said to them, on many occasions: "This time it will be different," or "I'm going to stop forever, I promise." So, they may not be ready to believe you when you say this, one more time. Perhaps a more useful way to approach this conversation is to honestly let them know what you're doing to support your recovery. You can be compassionate about the fact that it may take time for them to commence to trust you again.

Engaging in Safe Community

Whether you're just coming out of an addiction, are in recovery, or are new to spirituality, one key to creating safety is surrounding yourself with like-minded and like-hearted people. Being part of what I call an "intentional community"—a group of people dedicated to a shared intention—truly can support your recovery. That's why 12-step programs work so well for many people coming out of an addiction—there is a shared intention of sobriety. There's a shared intention of supporting each other in moving from addiction to recovery. And these days there are countless communities to choose from, no matter where you are in your recovery process.

Whatever you're seeking, whatever your aim in life, surrounding yourself with other people who share that intention can be an incredibly powerful tool. For one thing, it can assist with accountability, which gets you back to trusting yourself and others. And again, this doesn't mean accountability as in telling one another when you are doing something "wrong." Accountability in an intentional community is a matter of creating a wonderful mirror where you can reflect to one another in an uplifting and supportive way. To me that's the beauty of spiritual community.

For example, at Agape Bay Area, our spiritual center in Oakland, we have a shared intention of recognizing our essential nature and of seeing each other through the lens of oneness. We are accountable to one another in this shared intention. If one of us forgets our wholeness and perfection, we have these companions who are beautiful mirrors, reflecting that wholeness and perfection back to us. And whenever we need to look deeper, into something that's in shadow for us, we have companions who have been there before us, who can assure us that we are safe. To me, this shared intentionality accelerates the recovery process, the awakening process. Of course, spiritual communities are not immune to experiencing conflict. But that's not because we are essentially broken; it's because conflict can be a great source of our individual and collective evolution. What looks like conflict in community can be a healthy sign that we are holding each other accountable.

It can be a healthy sign that we're growing. Because, as we've seen, as long as we remain in our comfort zone, nothing changes.

Expanding Your Comfort Zone

I had a great spiritual teacher early on in my path who would say to me, "If you think you're doing well, you might not be. If you think you're not doing well, you probably are." I needed to hear that because staying in my comfort zone felt safe and I didn't want to leave it. But as long as I stayed there, I wasn't evolving. So yes, sometimes spiritual growth involves being uncomfortable because expanding our conscious awareness beyond what we currently recognize can be disorienting and sometimes even painful.

So, supportive community creates safety for us because its shared intentionality keeps us accountable, it allows us to look at the shadow places with people who love us and want us to develop, and it is a place where even conflict is a safe and productive thing, rather than something that will injure or threaten us. Spiritual community also fosters compassion. If we're walking through an addiction, healthy spiritual community will help us learn to receive compassion from others and feel compassion for ourselves and those around us. Compassion helps us to look at what's working rather than focusing on what seems to be broken. As Pema Chödrön writes, "*When you open yourself to the continually changing, impermanent, dynamic nature of your own being and of reality, you increase your capacity to love and care about other people and your capacity to not be afraid. You're able to keep your eyes open, your heart open, and your mind open.*"

Chapter Five

UNLEARNING

It's time to come back from the world of illusion, the world of lies, and return to your own truth, to your own authenticity. It's time to unlearn the lies and become the real you. And in order to do that, you need to come back to life, which is truth. Awareness is the key to coming back to life...where you rebel against all the lies that are ruling your head. You rebel, and the whole dream starts changing.
—Don Miguel Ruiz & Don Jose Ruiz, The Fifth Agreement

In this chapter, we'll continue the conversation about breaking free from the cycle of addiction, which is the continual search for an outside solution to remedy or numb something that feels broken internally. In chapter 4 we looked at the importance of creating a sense of safety. This chapter will offer you tools for uncovering and unlearning your core false beliefs, a process that involves the practice of self-parenting and the process of integrating the shadow. Through these spiritual practices, in an ongoing process of integration and wholeness, we can come to experience conscious awareness, what's called "witness consciousness," and a return to our essential selves.

Living Beyond Your Stories

It goes without saying that learning is important. The value we place on education is evident all around us: from educational leaders hailing it as the cornerstone of society, to politicians calling themselves "the education candidate" and business leaders saying we need a more sophisticated workforce. Yes, learning is empowering. When I was first introduced to spiritual teaching, I tried to learn as much as I possibly could about spiritual principles, about spiritual practices, about metaphysical laws and truths. All this was very valuable for me; I needed to learn in order to grow in consciousness. So why am I talking about the importance of unlearning? And, what are the stories we might need to live beyond?

When I was in my 20s and in early recovery, I was examining painful incidents of my past in order to resolve what still seemed unhealed. I remember calling my two sisters to have them corroborate the details of certain childhood happenings. To my surprise, they both recounted different versions of the same events, which seemed equally correct for each of them. It occurred to me that the three of us had three different yet equally real experiences of the same occurrences. We all had different experiences of our childhoods, and therefore we have created different stories about ourselves and the world at large. Because of this experience, I now realize that it is an important part of our spiritual development and recovery to question and live beyond the stories we have been carrying around about ourselves and the world, sometimes for years, maybe even decades.

With clear vision, we see that it no longer serves us to cling to *any* story that keeps us feeling stuck and limited. What would be the benefit of continuing to perpetuate stories that are not in alignment with the truth that we are *all* essentially whole? The fact that most of us are still living in a state of forgetfulness of that fundamental truth doesn't change that reality. As we shift our perspective about who and what we truly are, that in turn shifts the nature of the world we inhabit and our experience of others. The world becomes a more loving place because *we* have become more loving, openhearted human beings. And all we did was come into alignment with what was already true. This is what it means to live beyond our stories—about ourselves, others, and the world.

Evidence or Conclusion?

Most of us are taught that we come to a conclusion by gathering evidence. If we look at the "facts" of a situation, we will be able to determine the correct conclusion. Our entire legal system is based on this, and many in the scientific community adhere to this structure of knowing as well. I invite you to turn that concept on its head and begin to question this assumption. Is it possible that the reverse of this formula is actually true? Perhaps we come to a conclusion and then go about finding evidence to support that conclusion. This is often the case in our legal system, and quantum physics is now revealing this reality in the scientific field as well. The observer has an effect. In our personal lives, we may encounter situations which repeat themselves over and over. We can look to evidence to support our position. Or, we can pause and examine our conclusions and see what happens when we focus on changing them instead. Miraculous changes occur simply by looking at our assumptions and making the inner shift to a different way of seeing the world.

If we decide that some things in life are "good," and some are "bad," then we find ourselves living in a dualistic world where we need to be careful and keep ourselves safe. In this reality, things can go wrong, people can be hurtful, and we need to protect ourselves from those who want to harm us and from the evils of life. We can find plenty of evidence to confirm this reality. We don't necessarily need to ignore the world around us. In the end though, it is up to each of us to decide what kind of world we live in. We don't need to wait for anything to change on the outside before we can inhabit the world of our choice. What kind of world are you choosing to see today?

We can choose to recognize that everything that happens is useful for our recovery, and that it contributes to our well-being and our wholeness. We can step into in a world where nothing is actually against us. In this reality, there are no enemies. It is safe to befriend the here and now, and we can trust that whatever is happening in this moment can serve our highest spiritual development. Whatever happened in our past also served our highest spiritual awareness. In this way, we can have a daily living experience of being *at one with* the rest of life. We can know ourselves as part of the seamless fabric of existence. In fact, this is the only way we can experience our oneness with all that is, and tap into the profound sense of peace and harmony that already exists deep within us. *Letting go of our stories is the shortcut to living in a peaceful world.*

Relative Reality or Ultimate Reality?

Many metaphysical and mystical traditions make a distinction between relative reality and ultimate reality. Relative reality is everything we experience through our senses; it is anything that depends on something else; it is anything that changes. It's what we tend to call "the real world." Relative reality on the level of our individual personality is all our inner infrastructure—the structures of the ego; our ideas, beliefs, and points of view about ourselves and about life. It is what makes sense to us and works for us at any given point in our life journey. As we grow and learn, our relative reality changes. We let go of old things that no longer serve us and gravitate to new things that now seem more solid and more true. In other words, as we grow up, we develop new ways of seeing ourselves and the world. We adopt new perspectives.

Ultimate reality, on the other hand, does not change. It is beyond ego, personality, and experience. Ultimate reality, as revealed to us in spiritual traditions and practices, is just that; ultimate. Within ultimate reality lies the truth that we are born whole and perfect and absolutely one with Source. That deep perfection is the fundamental truth of who and what we are. We might call this God consciousness or our spiritual selves. Let me reiterate something here that we have discussed in earlier chapters: Within ultimate reality, we are ultimately and fundamentally whole and perfect. But this perfection does not mean that we are free from limitation (in relative reality) and it doesn't mean that we don't make what seems like mistakes. Our essential and fundamental wholeness does not mean we never will *feel* broken, or never *feel* hurt. Our mistakes and limitations may feel real, but they are only part of relative reality. Our brokenness, hurts, and wounded selves might feel real too. But they are only real at the level of relative reality.

This description of ultimate reality as something greater than our day-to-day lives might seem too abstract, so I'll delve more deeply into this concept. Many of us don't have the tools to recognize this oneness with the eternal, and even if we do glimpse it from time to time, we might not know what to do with it. Think about it: Have you ever had a spiritual experience? Have you ever felt one with nature, or with all humankind, or with all existence? Probably you have. That's not an anomaly—it's a connection with ultimate reality.

Many people, grounded as they are in the material, tangible world, might look at this sort of experience as a random event, as the result of some phenomenon in the brain. Or, they might dismiss it altogether. That doesn't mean it doesn't exist; it just means they didn't recognize it. But when we evolve spiritually, when we have undertaken spiritual practices that open our eyes to this ultimate reality, then we can be ready for it when it presents itself. That's what happened to me on that small boat on the Ganges, in the experience I described in the preface. Because I was open to and more or less prepared for that experience, it initiated a profound shift in my perception instead of passing by me unnoticed. In a way, it was a free gift, but I had also prepared myself to receive it in some way.

Of the two, relative reality and ultimate reality, most of us are primarily aware of relative reality—it's where we live our lives. But we are created in and strive to return to the unchanging dimension within ourselves. As we become more grounded in ultimate reality, we come to see more clearly that the truths of relative reality are fleeting. They change. When we are children, we seem to have an innate sense of ultimate reality, but then we begin to forget. And, quite literally, we get it "taught out" of us. So, for me, the spiritual journey and recovery are about unlearning.

There comes a point when it's time for us to unlearn the stories, the beliefs, the ideas that we have collected and internalized—stories that at one point may have seemed true but that are no longer fitting our lives. As we begin to awaken to a deeper reality, we begin to recognize that although we might call those stories "true," that truth lies only in relative reality. The key to living in peace and wholeness is moving beyond our stories. So, what are the truths, the stories, that once served you but are now keeping you stuck in a limited way of being?

Moving Beyond Limitation

I'm not asking you what you can do or what you can acquire that will make things OK. That's an old habit for many of us with addictions and addictive behaviors. Many of us believe that if we just look a certain way or act a certain way, if we can just get a certain person to respond to us in a certain way, all will be fine. This is different. Instead of looking for something outside ourselves to make things better, here we're looking inward and taking an honest look at the stories that keep us feeling stuck. What do I mean by "stuck?" Well, if you've been in recovery for any length of time you've probably spent some time looking at your life: your relationships, your attitudes, your patterns. Where do you seem to experience the same kinds of situations in your life, the same types of relationships over and over again, the same frustrations? Have you noticed a repetitive pattern?

Here's a story that represents this well: In the 1960s, a rare white Bengal tiger arrived at the National Zoo in Washington, D.C. The tiger, named Mohini, was a special gift to President Eisenhower and the people of America from the government of India. Mohini was placed in a temporary 12 x 12–foot cage, while the zoo discussed plans to build her a magnificent enclosure. The enclosure was to resemble her natural habitat, with lush forests, rolling hills, and everything a tiger could possibly need or want. During the construction period, Mohini paced around her cramped cage, in a figure-8 pattern, day after day. Unexpected delays in building the new habitat turned months into years, as the young tiger continued to pace around her small cage.

Finally, Mohini's new, spacious enclosure was completed and a large crowd gathered to witness the big event. At long last, she would be able to experience her freedom. To the crowd's great surprise, however, on entering her new home, Mohini headed straight to the far corner and started pacing around in the same figure-8 pattern, just as she had been forced to do for several years. Sadly, she spent the rest of her life in the small far corner of her enclosure, moving in the same figure-8, 12 x 12 pattern, completely oblivious to the paradise surrounding her. This story illustrates what happens when we allow our earlier programming to dictate the limits of our awareness and of our experience of life. My question to you is: What is *your* self-imposed, 12 x 12, figure-8 pattern? How are you living within the confines of an inherited belief system that still appears to be "real" for you? The truth is that you have the capacity to experience infinite freedom from within. You live in an infinitely abundant universe. It is only the limitations of your thinking, and the stories you tell yourself, that keep you tightly contained in a life that might feel smaller than you would like it to be.

So again, my question for you is, what self-imposed corners are you squeezed into in right now, what crazy-eight pattern are you stuck in? That pattern may have originally been a brilliant strategy that worked to support or protect you, but maybe now you're beginning to feel that something about it is just not adequate. What would it be like to expand your consciousness and open to the possibility of a different perspective? You've looked at these stories and beliefs before, in working through previous chapters; they are your core false beliefs. They are the fundamental beliefs about yourself that are getting in your way. When you uncover these beliefs, you may find that they are usually some variation on "I am ..." or "I am not ..."—for example, "I am unlovable," "I am stupid," "I am a disaster," or "I am not worthy," "I am not creative." And as we've seen in part 1, if you believe there's something fundamentally wrong with you, then that is the lens through which you will perceive life. You will then become attracted to relationships and situations, and you attract situations and relationships, that seem to confirm your belief. It's self-fulfilling.

The great news is that you don't have to *force* yourself to unlearn your core false beliefs. You don't even necessarily have to learn a new set of beliefs (although this can be one powerful way to work with these negative beliefs). The first step is simply recognizing that these are beliefs set in relative reality, not ultimate reality. They are changeable, not set in stone. Once you recognize that, you can begin to question them and, ultimately, let them go. As a wise teacher once said, the first step is awareness, the second step is awareness, and the third step is awareness.

Self-Parenting

One way to look at your core false beliefs is to pay attention to the messages you've received from the world throughout your life. For we are all walking around with an inner dialogue, a specific, personal, unique way of looking at the world that started when we were born, maybe even before. One of the ways that we express our unique perspective is through what's called "self-talk." It is the way that we communicate with ourselves internally, especially the way we talk with the parts of ourselves that feel wounded. I imagine some of your self-talk is kind and loving, and some of it is less so. Perhaps much of your self-talk is grounded in your core false beliefs.

One valuable tool in unlearning self-talk that no longer serves us is through the beneficial practice of self-parenting. In self-parenting, we learn to talk, in a loving and supportive way, to those parts of ourselves that feel wounded. We learn to parent the small inner child that may have experienced trauma or that may be sitting in toxic shame, the self that feels disconnected and broken. This is the kind of parenting that maybe we didn't get as small children, and fortunately, we can provide it to ourselves as adults. Many of us were not raised with the type of communication, in either words or actions, that helped us to grow and thrive. And it was this lack of conscious parenting, in part, that gave us our core false beliefs. When there's abuse early in life or an experience of abandonment, the core false beliefs that often result include things like, "Life is not safe," "I can't feel this right now," and "You're going to leave me."

Some of us got the message that it isn't OK to make mistakes or it isn't OK to feel what some might refer to as negative emotions. Some of us got the message that there is a right way and a wrong way: if I'm a good child, I get rewarded (or at least I don't get hurt); if I'm a bad child, I get punished. If we hold these limiting beliefs as adults, we will most likely never learn how to enrich our emotional lives, how to question things, even how to comfort ourselves.

Self-parenting is another way of unlearning ideas and constructs that no longer serve us. We do this by replacing the negative self-talk with supportive and loving self-talk to create a place of safety internally. In assisting people with self-parenting, I have found three key phrases to be incredibly simple and powerful. These are things we say to ourselves in self-parenting: (1) You're safe now, (2) It's OK to feel this way now, and (3) I'm here for you now. So, let's go through these and see how they can help in the unlearning process.

You're safe now.

Part of conscious parenting is keeping our children safe. This is not about keeping them insulated from anything and everything that might harm them; it's about teaching them to be independent and resilient in whatever circumstances they find themselves. This involves creating or finding safe places for them, places of psychological safety as well as physical safety. Unfortunately, not all of us had that kind of parenting. Early in our lives, many of us were taught—either consciously or unconsciously, sometimes covertly and sometimes very overtly—that it's not safe for us to be who and what we are. This sense of insecurity can cause a profound separation from our essential nature. We've worked with this earlier, especially in chapters 1 and 3, on unresolved trauma and toxic shame. So, part of self-parenting is being able to talk to ourselves as we would to our child, reassuring ourselves that all is well. When we self-parent, we can say to ourselves in times of crisis or difficulty, "You're safe. It's safe to be you right now. It's safe to be exactly as you are."

It's OK to feel this way now.

Very simply said, addiction can be framed as a response to the fear of feeling, the fear of being right here, right now. Addictive behavior is what we do to avoid being in the present. So at first, telling ourselves "It's OK to feel this way right now" might feel quite foreign. If we have a core belief that we are unsafe, then the idea that it's safe to get in touch with what we're feeling on an emotional level might seem very challenging or untrue. But emotional awareness is very important for those of us in recovery, and so it helps to literally give ourselves the message that it's safe to look within: "It's OK to feel this way right now." As we come further into our spiritual practice and our recovery, we begin to thaw out, to start feeling things we had been ignoring or avoiding or not allowing ourselves to feel, and this deepening becomes more comfortable and less threatening. If you are finding yourself challenged by these feelings, you might want to start by saying "something in me feels…" rather than "I feel…" as this can assist you in getting in touch with the emotion without getting flooded or overwhelmed.

I'm here for you now.

At the core of a lot of our anxiety is the belief that "If I let you truly see me, you will leave." The root of this core false belief may have been a result of parenting that was judgmental, abusive, emotionally distant, or love that was conditional on our behavior. With this self-parenting phrase, "I'm here for you now," we're genuinely giving ourselves the parenting that maybe we didn't get growing up. We're dedicating ourselves *to* ourselves, committing ourselves to being there for ourselves as we would hope to be there for a child, or a life partner. As Tracy McMillan put it in her TEDx talk, *"You enter a relationship with yourself, and then you put a ring on it. In other words, you commit to yourself fully.... Loving myself exactly where I am, is the only way to get where I'm going."*

Again, here are the three phrases you can start saying to yourself to begin a healthy inner dialogue: "You're safe now," "It's OK to feel this way now," and "I'm here for you now." If you can practice these three things and begin to use them any time you feel anxious, sad, etc. you'll find a new way of being with yourself.

Recognizing the Shadow

In psychological terms, the shadow is the unconscious aspect of yourself, that you keep hidden due to a desire to repress the seemingly negative attributes of your personality. An important element of your recovery work is looking at and integrating the shadow: those parts of yourself that you have buried beneath the surface, beneath your conscious awareness, those parts of yourself that you may not want to see or express. The shadow is what you hold shame about—your unresolved trauma, your fragmented self. You conceal those parts in the shadow, and because they're repressed and not integrated, they tend to surface in ways that make you feel out of control. Renowned psychologist, Carl Jung stated this so simply when he said: *"Until you make the unconscious conscious, it will direct your life and you will call it fate."* And, once you bring the shadow into conscious awareness, you recognize you can begin choosing, rather than being run by your unconscious programming.

Let's take an example. Nadia holds a core belief that others will not value her if she does anything that she considers to be wrong. We can look to her childhood for the roots of this belief, but I think you can imagine where it comes from. This belief leads her to bury in the shadow her true fear: that she is deeply imperfect and wholly unlovable. Whenever this thought or the feelings associated with it come up, Nadia panics and does whatever she can to shove them back down. Sometimes this results in behavior that is damaging to her relationships. Say Nadia's husband points out something she's doing that irritates him. Quite often this will cause her, without thinking, to turn the tables on him in a way that's aggressive and unfair. So, if he says something like, "Honey, would you mind not turning the light on when you come to bed after I'm asleep?" she might respond, lightning quick, with something like, "What? How do you expect me to find things in the dark? Why do you go to bed so early anyway? It's like you don't want to be around me. I so don't need this when I'm tired and trying to get ready to finally relax!"

Nadia inevitably regrets her reaction, explaining it by saying that she has no control over her temper. That is one way to look at it, and Nadia might address her problem with anger management therapy or medication. If we look at it from a spiritual perspective, however, we will see that her expressions of anger result from a cascade of consequences stemming from her spiritual disconnection. Early in life, Nadia became disconnected from the truth of who she is and she bought into some core false beliefs about herself as broken and unlovable. Because this perspective of herself brings with it feelings that are too terrible to bear, she buries and represses her sense of worthlessness, which in turn tends to come out in unexpected and damaging ways, erupting in these explosions of anger and projections of worthlessness onto those around her.

So, Nadia is trapped in the corner of her own worthlessness, and she projects that, unconsciously, onto others. If she holds onto that story, that core false belief in her own worthlessness, her ability to move freely will be limited. The shadow will seem to be controlling her life, directing her actions and determining what feels fundamentally true to her (like the idea that she cannot control her temper). So, in addition to working with her doctor and her therapist on ways to manage her anger, Nadia can also grow spiritually by examining, in a safe place, what lies in her shadow, bringing it to the surface and working to integrate that into the light of day.

Stuck in the Shadow

When we bring what's in the shadow into conscious awareness, we start to recognize that we have a choice, that the shadow does not have to run our lives. Again, a shift in awareness is key here. If we believe that our perspective of the world is the ultimate truth, that there's no additional way of seeing things, then life is going to be something that's happening *to* us. But once we commence to recognize that everything we see outside of ourselves is merely a projection of our inner reality, things will begin to shift. When we reframe our stories, things change.

In your previously held stories, the things in your shadow—your perceived flaws and imperfections, your secret sorrows, your triggers—look like ultimate reality and so they seem to have control; you believe you are their victim. You hold the beliefs that underlie your shadow as if they were absolute truths. But if you acknowledge that these viewpoints are not the fundamental truth, you can bring the story into the realm of conscious awareness. Then you can start to see your shadow as something other than a dictator and to recognize your own power. But, you might ask: "If my shadow resides in my unconscious, how do I make the unconscious, conscious?"

Integrating the Shadow

If you've committed yourself to working through these chapters, I trust that by now you've come a long way. You've started to genuinely internalize the fact that your story is only one way of looking at things, that life is not what's happening *to* you but what you're *calling* it. You've begun to make that shift in awareness, to see that everything that's happening in the outer realm is actually a reflection of your inner consciousness rather than reality.

I trust that you've started to examine where your stories came from, where you got those core false beliefs that are no longer working for you. You've begun to question the source of where you developed your ideas and assumptions about what you call life. And you're on your way to recognizing and integrating the shadow. If you feel like you're not there yet, I invite you to put that doubt aside for now and simply sit in gratitude for the growth that's already occurred and that is continuing to occur.

As you begin to work with your shadow, it's important to appreciate the need for safety. Because the shadow can sometimes be painful. Again, renowned psychologist Carl Jung stated it so beautifully when he said: *"There is no coming to consciousness without pain. People will do anything, no matter how absurd, in order to avoid facing their own Soul. One does not become enlightened by imagining figures of light, but by making the darkness conscious."* Illuminating and integrating your shadow material requires a sense of inner security and trust. Certainly, your inner work of self-love and acceptance, as well as any work you do with a therapist or spiritual counselor, can help in nurturing safety and recognizing what's happening in the shadow. Meditation and other awareness practices are also useful tools. Once you are open to them, insights will come up while you're journaling, walking, or even singing in the shower.

These are relatively solitary practices, and it can be tempting to keep our shadow work to ourselves. But keep in mind that creating safety also involves community. We keep our shadow selves hidden in part because we think no one else would understand, because we're ashamed to admit them to others. But the fact is, everyone has "stuff" in their shadow. And chances are, your shadow looks a lot like your neighbor's shadow. So once you've recognized what's in the shadow, community can help you integrate that shadow fully into your conscious awareness. This, of course, is not always a linear process. Part of the strategy of creating community is nurturing relationships in which it's safe to speak genuinely. For example, "I always say I'm fine because I'm afraid to admit I'm not," "I'm secretly sitting on a huge pile of rage," or "I'm afraid I don't know what love is." Every time you say such things out loud in a safe place, with people you trust and in a spirit of self-love and acceptance, they hold less power over you.

Another way to shift things so they lose their power over you, is to play with your shadow. Try, for instance, to imagine your shadow as something other than menacing. Can you see your shadow as a teacher? What can you learn from it? If your shadow holds anger, can that anger teach you something about what lies beneath it? Can you see your shadow as a beloved child? How can you show it love and concern? If your shadow holds your innermost sorrow, can you comfort it? I know that being in the presence of these "shadowy" things can seem daunting. But you have more courage than you may realize. You might just need a little encouragement, and the shadow realm is a good place to put it into practice.

Raising Your Conscious Awareness

Here is a wonderful quote from Deepak Chopra: *"I've worked all my life on the subject of awareness, whether it's awareness of the body, awareness of the mind, awareness of your emotions, awareness of your relationships, or awareness of your environment. I think the key to transforming your life is to be aware of who you are."*

There is a great story about how we can shift our awareness

and therefore change how we experience what we call reality. It is a story about two different dogs. Both, at separate times, walk into the same room. One comes out wagging her tail. The other one comes out growling. A woman watching this goes into the room to see what could possibly make one dog so happy and the other one so mad. To her surprise, she finds a room filled with the mirrors. The happy dog found a thousand happy dogs looking back at her while the angry dog saw only angry dogs growling back at him. What you *see* in the world around you is a reflection of who you are and the feeling tone you are holding. Once we know that, we can begin to shift the "stories" we are telling about ourselves and the world and therefore begin to change our life experiences.

Awareness is a marvelous gift of healing that has many levels. As we begin to raise our conscious awareness, we give ourselves permission to feel and create a safe space where our wounding can see the light of day. We become aware of the lens through which we're looking at the world, we become aware of our core false beliefs. We become aware of our thoughts, our inner dialogue. We become aware of what's in the shadow, all the unconscious self-talk and the shaming and shameful patterning that has been influencing our conscious decisions. We become aware of the level of consciousness from which we are operating and we begin to return to our original perfection. And from this space of recognizing our oneness with the essential self, we can witness even more fully our ego, our shadow, our humanity. And, there are always deeper levels of awareness.

Activating Intentionality

In part, conscious awareness is about becoming attentive to our thoughts and intentions. But awareness can go beyond our thoughts and our intentions, to an understanding of the deeper energy that we are holding about ourselves and the world. That feeling tone, is what actually creates reality, because it holds a particular frequency. This is not to say that awareness of our thoughts and our intentions is unnecessary. After all, what I'm calling our feeling tone is created in part by our inner dialogue—the language of our thoughts, what we say to ourselves and others about the world. As we've seen, if we have unresolved trauma, if we carry toxic shame, if we are disconnected spiritually, then our inner dialogue may be negative and unconscious.

If that's the case, then growing in awareness means becoming more conscious of that language and the stories we live by, recognizing how we are caught in a way of seeing the world that is based on some fundamental lies we have about ourselves. That's the level of awareness that I've been focusing on so far in this book. The process of deepening awareness on the level of language and intentionality involves changing how we think about ourselves and the world. As we become aware at this level, we pay attention to how our intentionality affects our outer life. "This self-critical language blocks me," or "If I hold this thought it's going to manifest in my world." This level of awareness helps free us from a victim consciousness, as you may have experienced.

When I was first introduced to metaphysical teachings, I needed to focus on deepening this level of awareness. And I thought that was all there was to it. It seemed to me that spiritual development was *only* about changing my mind and therefore changing my reality. As I learned and grew, I was able to identify my negative inner dialogue and consciously choose my thoughts, to be more aware on that level. In other words, I focused on growing in awareness of my intentionality, without realizing I could go deeper. But, that awareness wasn't enough to change my reality because I was still carrying a negative feeling tone about myself. In my mind, I believed in my essential wholeness, but I wasn't convinced of it in my heart and body. I still held

the core false beliefs at the level of my being. And this feeling
tone about myself was more powerful than my thoughts; it was
actually creating the vibration at which I was living and it was
forming what we call reality. Yes, I did need to become aware of
my thoughts and intentions, but I needed to go deeper as well.
Thoughts do play a great role in recovery because if we're having
negative inner dialogue, our feeling tone isn't going to change.
But the process of unlearning and letting go also involves resting
in a deeper level of beingness, and transforming our feeling tone.

Sometimes this shift comes to us all at once or in a great leap,
as in a profound spiritual experience or in a dream. As you might
remember from my personal story in the preface, I had such an
experience on the Ganges—in which my ego seemed to be stripped
away and I experienced only love and oneness. This experience
created a real shift in my feeling tone, in my deepest awareness.
Of course, that experience ended, and I returned to my "regular"
life. I left India and came home, to work, finances, relationships,
etc. And on the surface, nothing seemed to have changed. There
was no miracle cure to all my day-to-day life. Spiritual experiences
do not suddenly make everything miraculously shift in the outer
world, at least not right away.

But that doesn't mean that what happened wasn't real. That
doesn't mean that my experience was simply the result of a chemical
reaction. Something powerful had happened; there had been a
profound change. Even though I still experienced all the "stuff"
I had left behind when I went to India, even though my ego still
crept back, that experience had initiated a permanent shift in the
way I *related* to ego, the way I *framed* my story, the way I interpreted
what you might call my wounding. And what I comprehend now,
or what I'm understanding now at a deeper level, is this: These
profound experiences, grounded in our inner work and spiritual
practice, can bring us to a level where we can witness all our old

stories, difficulties, and ego from an awareness of ultimate reality. Spiritual experiences like the one I had in India can help us experience our essential selves, unharmed and unharmable. This is what we call "witness consciousness."

Becoming the Observer

As we come to remember and to know the highest truth of who we are, we experience ourselves as the ultimate observer of all things. In meditation, we no longer identify with or try to control our mind. Rather we simply bring our awareness to that truest part of ourselves, the energy field of our inner essence. We witness all things in our life through the eyes of compassion and understanding. Knowing ourselves *as* those qualities allows us to *be* that in the world. We no longer need to wait or expect somebody else to demonstrate those qualities in our lives. We *become* the model of it, demonstrating to others the possibility of living in peace and harmony, here and now. No waiting is required. We become a living example to others that it is safe to live openheartedly in this world.

At this mystical level of living, there is no longer any desire or need to blame, judge, or to make others wrong. And if we do momentarily forget who we are, we can easily find our way back to *being* love. We understand and have compassion for the human condition. We see that the vast majority of people are still trapped in a limited, separate identity. They have forgotten their true nature. They are a potential danger to themselves and to others. Coming from a place of separation and fear, they believe they live in a dangerous world. When their safety feels threatened, they are convinced there is no alternative but to attack others in order to preserve their well-being. This way of being currently plagues humanity. The phrase—*"Forgive them, for they know not what they have done"*—comes to mind. We might add to this by saying *"Forgive them, for they know not who they are."* How could they know, when they have assumed a false identity?

The Joy of Beingness

Conscious Recovery is about who you are *being* in addition to what you are doing. What we're talking about is tapping into a new way of being, and that involves creating a safe space, that involves unlearning, that involves deepening our awareness to come ever closer to that space within us that is absolutely whole and perfect and one with the universe. As Michael Beckwith said, *"Energy doesn't get created, we just find a new way of moving it."* So, we're really talking about tapping into essential energy.

Let's say we're unhappy with "what's happening in our life." If we are unaware of our inner dialogue, we might put these events into the story that fits our core false beliefs: "This is just like everything else in my life because nothing good ever happens to me," or "This happened because I'm a failure," or whatever. As we become more aware of our inner dialogue, we may get better at recognizing our stories and we may start to let go of them. But we may still tend to judge what's happening, to assign blame and try to identify what needs to be "fixed." Even if we are aware on an intentional level, judgment can creep in: "I can't believe I manifested this. What's wrong with me that I haven't been able to change this pattern?" And as we've seen, judgment solidifies the old way of being. If we're unhappy with what we're seeing in the manifest realm, what helps more than judgment is an awareness that's without judgment. Self-love and self-acceptance can help move our awareness from the level of thought to the level of beingness.

When you're faced with illness or loss or some other difficulty, I invite you to look within and ask not only, "What am I saying about this? What am I thinking about this?" but also, "What am I feeling about this? At what vibration or frequency am I holding about this?" Do this from a place of self-love and acceptance. Judgment of anything that you discover when you ask these questions only blocks your growth and your awareness. As Krishnamurti said, *"The highest form of human intelligence is the ability to see ourselves without evaluating, without judgment."* By being willing to look within and ask what thoughts, what beliefs, what energy we are holding about ourselves and the world, we can move to a deeper level of conscious awareness.

The tendency to slip back into our stories and to judge may not immediately disappear with deepening awareness. What does shift is that these things become less habitual. As our awareness deepens, we're more likely to recognize our inner dialogue and our judgment as signs that we need to look more deeply at something. As we become more aware, we're able to see what's truly happening. For most of us, this is an ever-evolving process. We are always expanding. I don't think we grow spiritually so much as we grow in awareness of our spiritual self. It's not a linear process, from A to Z. Nor is it a circular process, simply repeating stages of growth over and over. It's more of a spiral process because we move through levels of consciousness, from A to B to C in an ever upward movement. As we grow in awareness, we inevitably return to similar situations in our lives, not in mere repetition, but in a new way of considering them from a higher level of consciousness that we have attained. And this changes everything.

Through our awareness we transform how we experience what happens. So, our reality is created by our response to what happens; how we describe what happens, how we interpret what happens, the stories we tell about what happens, and how we feel internally about what happens. As we become more aware on all these levels, we experience deeper transformation. The more we let go, the more we return to our essential selves.

And the more we dismantle our core false beliefs, the more we come to a feeling tone of our essential nature. As we tap into that ultimate vibration of who we *genuinely* are, life cannot help but manifest all around us in accordance with that vibration, in accordance with our beingness. And that's very different than holding thoughts and believing that thoughts *alone* create manifestation in the outer realm.

I remember a conversation I heard at Agape Bay Area, our spiritual center in Oakland, some time ago. Someone had asked the question: "Is the intention to heal our wounds?" It is such a great question, because on one level of consciousness, we could say, "Of course it's about doing the work of healing. Of course, it's about recognizing and attending to our losses, brokenness, and wounding." And then there's this other level, this witness consciousness, from where we recognize that our essential self is unharmed and unharmable. It's a self that knows no wounding, and thus requires no healing.

When we tap into that consciousness, we create a connection with our essential selves, we deepen that oneness with the Source that we are, and the question about healing becomes almost irrelevant. I want to be careful here because I'm not saying that there's either healing or no healing. It's not either/or—it's both/and. So, of course, we do the work of healing the wounds; that work seems necessary. Without that inner work, we might not truly recognize and benefit from the spiritual experiences when they happen. That inner work helps us get to the place of witness consciousness; it leads us to the recognition that nothing needs to change for us to be complete or lovable or happy. Nothing at all needs to change in the outer realm because we have connected with and recognized, our oneness with Source.

Chapter Six

PRACTICING SPIRITUAL PRINCIPLES

Someone may first take interest in spiritual practice to improve her life. But practice doesn't just improve your life — it also newly defines the meaning of your life.... When anyone, anywhere, learns to abide in such loving wisdom, they generate a zone of refuge and protection that encircles all those around them. They become a force to remake this world into a place of deep mutual reverence and appreciation. To learn to embody such wise love, and to act from there for the sake of all, is the greatest gift we can give to our families, communities and world.

— *John Makransky*

In this chapter, I'd like to introduce you to some spiritual principles you can practice that will help you to break free of any kind of addiction and to live a more connected and awe-filled life. These principles are nonresistance, non-judgment, mindfulness, living in the question, and accepting impermanence. These spiritual principles are an important part of breaking free from addiction, and they can support you if you want to live a more connected, dynamic, and open-hearted life.

What is Nonresistance?

What comes up when you hear the word "nonresistance?" It might evoke images of surrender, giving up, or weakness. Nonresistance might seem counterintuitive and very different from the way you've framed your life thus far. This is possibly because in our culture we are taught to resist: we're taught to win, we're taught to compete, we're taught to never give up, and never surrender. At a deeper level, we're taught from a very early age to "make life happen." We're taught to shape our lives by manipulating our environment and, to some extent, the people around us. This creates a general posture of pushing, either toward or away from things.

We fight and push and strive because we're programmed to think of life through the lens of scarcity, which says that there isn't enough for everyone. This assumes that if we don't push, if we don't fight, if we don't manipulate, we won't get what we want or what we need. If we believe there is a limited amount of "stuff," then of course we're going to resist, of course we're going to fight, of course we're going to strive toward some things and avert from others.

This describes my experience perfectly. I spent much of my life trying to resist *what is*. When I came to metaphysical teachings in the late 80s, I even started using the spiritual principles I was learning as a method to manipulate the outer realm. For example, I loved the idea of using affirmations to create the life of my dreams. At that point in my awareness, this meant that if I could get the outside looking a certain way, then I would be OK internally. The litmus test, of course, is whether our approach is working. Does this strategy of resistance get us what we want? The decision to live by striving and struggle may work for a while to help us achieve what we desire. But as we become more aware, we are led to question the assumptions that ground that decision.

In my mid twenties, I went to India, where I spent several weeks with Amma (Mata Amritanandamayi), "the Hugging Saint." At one point, I asked her how to quit smoking, and she said, "Learn to love the cigarette." Startling advice! But, by that time I could agree that being *against* the smoking wasn't getting me anywhere. It was only producing more negative energy around my smoking. Amma helped me see that I could shift my perspective to one of nonresistance, and that helped me let go of the addictive habit. Once I stopped resisting the smoking I could begin to ask myself if I was still happy with myself as a smoker. I started to have love and compassion for myself, and I soon discovered that I could then more easily stop smoking. It seemed counterintuitive at the time, but I now understand that love and compassion are greater change agents than criticism and judgment.

How much time do you waste resisting the circumstances of your life, resisting the people in your life? And where does this get you? If you've been aware of your patterns for any length of time, the answer may be, "Not where you really want to go." So, what is nonresistance, and how do you practice it as a spiritual principle? Byron Katie defines nonresistance right in the title of her superb book *Loving What Is*. Nonresistance is loving *what is*, or at very least, it is accepting what is. It's absolute acceptance of this moment. When you practice nonresistance, you allow yourself to become aware of the natural flow of life, you surrender and let go. It's about opening up to being with whatever shows up in your outer realm, and in your inner experience as well, giving you a deeper understanding of what's really happening in your life *and* tapping into something that's far more powerful.

Practicing Nonresistance

One practice that can be a great doorway to nonresistance is to spend time in meditation. A meditation that focuses on witnessing *what is* can help us recognize our resistance and then let it go. This can be difficult at first. And when our every urge is to fight back, it takes great fortitude and courage to practice nonresistance. Fortunately, it's a power that can be implemented and strengthened. It's a practice that becomes easier with experience. When I was learning to meditate, I believed that the purpose of meditation was to quiet the mind. But that assumption was in itself a resistance of *what is*—I got very frustrated sitting on my pillow because I expected my mind to be quieted and it only seemed to get louder.

The power of meditation as a tool of nonresistance becomes evident when we shift our intention from trying to quiet the mind to witnessing and recognizing how we are in the world. We learn a great deal when we simply sit with our thoughts— not in *judgment*, but in *observation*. As meditation teaches us how to notice our thoughts, we also come to notice where we're stuck and to recognize those places where we might be resisting life. Thus, meditation can be a method for looking within and tapping into that deepest, truest part of ourselves, and from there witnessing how we are with what we might call our ego; our thoughts, emotions and perspectives. When we make that shift in our meditation practice, from a practice of trying to quiet the mind to a practice of witnessing and being curious, we become much less frustrated. Now we can experience meditation as being curious about *what is*. Being curious with how we relate to the world. Being curious about our thoughts, our perspectives, our viewpoints. Flowing *with* rather than pushing *against*.

You may be concerned that the practice of nonresistance is a sign of weakness. Again, a shift in perspective will be beneficial here. We're taught from a young age that vulnerability, authenticity, and the willingness to be intimate are weaknesses. Men especially are taught to have all the answers, and to use force to get what we think we need. But this is not strength. On the contrary, what we think of as strength is often a manifestation of fear—think of the playground bully who is, underneath all his bravado, often bullied himself and thus full of fear. Real strength, real power, is about flowing with life, being absolutely present, and curious about where the ship of life might want to take us. It's about gently *steering* the ship rather than forcing it through the water.

As we've seen in previous chapters, life is more about what we call it than about what's actually "happening." Nonresistance is a spiritual principle that allows us to truly experience this truth. By giving us practice in noticing our thoughts and perspectives, nonresistance allows us to see that our stories are not the complete picture, that our assumptions might be broadened, that our strategies might be improved. Practicing nonresistance in the inner realm, as in meditation, prepares us to exercise nonresistance in the outer realm.

We may have come into our journeys believing our opinions to be fact, believing our perspectives and core beliefs to be "the way the world is" or "just the way things are." And our beliefs tend to get reinforced by our experiences, and get solidified. When we live from a place of resistance, that resistant energy tends to feed the thing we're resisting. As previously mentioned, "What we resist persists." When we're holding the energy of resistance, competition, or scarcity, that energy attracts more of that energy. "We can't plant an elm seed and get a maple tree," as another saying goes. If we're holding resistance and anger, we're just going to experience more of that.

But, when we develop curiosity, we start noticing our thoughts, ideas, perspectives, and viewpoints, and we can begin to recognize that they aren't as solid as we once believed. In other words, through the practice of nonresistance, through the practice of witnessing our thoughts, we can actually recognize those places where we are choosing a perspective that may not be the whole story. For most of us, these perspectives are constructed from some story from the past, some belief that has become hardened in our consciousness. Nonresistance allows us to take a broader view and ask ourselves, "What am I choosing right now? Is it possible to see this differently?" Once we let go of resisting, it feels like we can enter the flow of existence, to move *with* life rather than *against* it.

In terms of addiction, the practice of nonresistance allows us to let go of the negative energy that's associated with our addictive behavior and attend to what lives underneath. When we let something go, it no longer has power in our lives. Further, when we do our inner work of letting go—which is acceptance of what is, even *loving* what is—that affects the collective. As more and more of us have the courage to practice nonresistance, what we see is a ripple effect in all aspects of life. Nonresistance is one of the most powerful spiritual principles that we can practice. As we become adept at it, we come to see that when we release our energy from the thing we've been resisting, we inevitably come to a place of peace and grace. If we're unhappy with something in our lives right now, we can start with nonresistance and acceptance.

What is Judgment?

Judgment can be seen as the opposite of love. When judgment is present, it cuts us off from love, or at the very least it confines love so that it can't fully reach us. Judgment is looking at the world in terms of "right" and "wrong;" it's a habit of approaching people and things and seeing them as "good" or "bad." Looking at this in terms of addiction, we can frame our judgmental habits of mind as an addiction to the need to be right. What's wrong with wanting to be right? What's wrong with judgment? We all do it, right? Usually we don't even think about it. If you're like most people, you might not even recognize that you are judging. In fact, most of us are constantly judging. We judge people and things, ideas and beliefs, situations and experiences, as attractive or unattractive, as positive or negative. Brain scientists have studied how we react to things—all kinds of things: random objects, common phrases, faces of different races—and they've found that we humans make snap judgments about lots of things. Some would even argue that we judge everything we encounter, that we are in a constant state of reaction to our surroundings. Science has shown that for approximately 97% of our lives, we are simply reacting habitually to our environment.

People tend to automatically evaluate things as they perceive them. You might see a certain food and get hungry. You might see someone doing something and you experience an emotion—you make a judgment, you react. You might even judge yourself: You react to your own looks or behavior with dismay, criticism, or arrogance. These gut reactions are lightning fast, and are for the most part unconscious and unintentional. This behavior is part of your *created* self; it has helped you survive. Have you ever felt judged by someone? On what basis did they get their information? Is it possible the judgment was more about them than you? As the saying goes: *"People will love you and people will hate you. And most of it will have very little to do with you."*

Again, the question is, does judgment really work? In my experience, judgment as a way of responding is a limited and limiting strategy when it's unconscious, when we don't see it for what it is. The problem is that our snap judgments create a predisposition for or against the thing or person perceived. They create bias. But because they are unconscious, we tend to trust these judgments like we trust our senses. They seem neutral or objective to us, when in fact they are not. Because our judgments are not neutral or objective, they are inherently limited; they are not the whole story. As such, they could be blinding us, keeping us from totally seeing the thing or person in front of us, from being fully present. And if our judgments are getting in the way of being wholly present, then they are also preventing us from experiencing love and connection.

Furthermore, when we're judging unconsciously and habitually, we're living and exemplifying duality. Those judgments and the decisions that come out of those judgments are based on a core belief that there truly is a right and a wrong, and so our feeling tone depends on where we fit into that scheme of things. In judging the world, we judge ourselves, trapping ourselves in this duality so that we must live either to be right or to be wrong. This keeps us feeling stuck in relative reality, rather than experiencing the oneness of ultimate reality. Fortunately, if we become conscious of our habits of judgment, we can change them. We do this first, by recognizing when we are judging; second, by evaluating the effect our judgment is having (does it work?); and third, by practicing nonjudgmental responses to our experience, ourselves, and the world. What happens when we do this? What happens when we shift from judgment to non-judgment?

Practicing Non-Judgment

Let's look at the first step here: recognizing our propensity to judge. This requires us to utilize the first practice in this chapter, nonresistance. By practicing and developing habits of nonresistance, we can identify and observe our judgments and then question whether they are working for us. As we saw a couple of sections ago, nonresistance is about becoming an observer instead of a reactor. It takes a lot of courage to remain nonresistant and thus to stay fully present. For most of us, this involves sitting and observing what our reactions are. This can be an external or an internal process, and it might be easier in some ways to start externally.

For instance, someone makes a remark to you. Practicing nonresistance, you can simply observe: How are you judging this situation? What is your judgment about this person? Then you can take that more deeply inward: You can observe what that statement activates or triggers internally. Maybe you feel a tightness in your throat or your chest or your stomach, maybe you experience the urge to react, to lash out, to judge. So you can observe your reaction, and recognize your desire to judge. And then you can go even deeper: What is your judgment about *yourself* in this moment? What are you saying about yourself when you judge this person or situation? What are you believing about yourself to be true?

Thus, we move to the second step, noticing the effect our judgment is having. What happens if you follow the path of judgment and criticize, or lash out, or move aggressively? Does your reaction or judgment work for you in this situation? What effect is your judgment having on your relationships, on your interactions, on your decisions? Does this move you closer to love and connection? As you question your own judgments and recognize their impact, you can move a step forward and come to a conscious decision for non-judgment. When you respond with non-judgment, you can take note of your response, and notice how its effect is different from that of a judgmental response. And on and on. The more you practice, the easier it gets.

What we discover as we go through this process is that judgment generally does not work. It confines our freedom. It stops us from remaining curious, from looking deeper, from appreciating what we're judging. And that decreases our capacity for love and connection. You might find that the definitions of rightness and wrongness you've been working with limit your freedom. You might find that they keep you stuck, and create barriers and separation. When we observe rather than react, when we sit with our triggers and identify where we most desire to judge, we often find that judgment of others is judgment about ourselves, it's a projection onto others of our shadow, our core beliefs about ourselves. That's why we gossip: It's a form of judgment that allows us to avoid what's happening internally. It lets us divert our attention from ourselves onto another. So, if you find that judgment is limiting for you, perhaps the next step is to wake up to the possibility of another way, a way that will lead you to your essential self. In this way, there is no judgment. There's only curiosity, acceptance, and connection.

Fortunately, through the practices of nonresistance, observation, being present and questioning, we can learn to give up our habits of judgment. We can learn to allow our triggers to go through us instead of taking control of us. That's how we come to the place in our essential self that's neutral, that's beyond judgment, beyond clinging to the fixed ideas and concepts we are holding about ourselves and the world. As we integrate our own shadow, as we let go of our own addictions, as we make peace with ourselves and recognize the love that we truly are, then that love becomes more what we perceive in others. We no longer enjoy gossip because it no longer serves us; our tendency to judge becomes more conscious and easier to discontinue. Our spiritual influences become stronger and non-judgment becomes our habit. And thus, it's possible within the practice of non-judgment that we can loosen the grip of our perspective and open to a greater way of being and seeing. Because, the ultimate truth of who and what we are is free of judgment. It is one with the ultimate power of the universe, and in that space, there is no judgment.

Developing Your Own Understanding of Spirit

I want to say a word to anyone who grew up with or who holds the belief that there is a judging higher power of some sort. Within this belief is the idea that there is only one spiritual or religious truth, that "there is no salvation outside my religion," or some variation of this. If this is what your sense of Spirit is, then you might ask yourself if it comes out of a worldview based on "right" or "wrong," "good" and "bad." A further question might be, how is it working for you? For instance, it's understandable that we can find reassurance in the idea of a "true belief system." If you find the "truth" in your religion and are comforted by it, then what you might truly be seeking is a structure that helps make sense of the world, a lens that tells you how to respond to your experience. And if your religion's truth offers you a way to judge your experience, and to judge other worldviews, from the confident ground of rightness, or "righteousness," then it can be reassuring in this irrational, complicated world. But is this belief system helping you to feel more grounded in love? Is it assisting you in experiencing deeper connections with yourself and others?

A need that lies further in the shadow might also be present in a dualistic sense of the divine, meaning the belief in a God or higher power that is "up there" and "out there" somewhere. When we are loaded down with toxic shame, when we have experienced trauma that is unresolved, when we carry core false beliefs that threaten to break our oneness with Spirit, a belief in a judgmental God or an exclusive religion might very well fit with our experience. If we believe we are essentially worthless, then a judging God can seem to give us some sense of salvation, but can also reinforce the belief in our unworthiness. If we feel that we are thoroughly and uniquely unlovable, then a religion that preaches a loving God but reveals a judging God will only confirm our feelings. In this case, our religion might provide more harm than help in our journey of recovery toward wholeness.

So, I invite you to examine your understanding of Spirit. Does your relationship assume a right/wrong, good/bad, us/them duality? If it does, what are you seeking in that duality? And, what are you finding there? Is the relationship working for you? Or are you using it to avoid something deeper? If you are coming up against the limits of your relationship with Spirit, then you might continue to practice the spiritual principles in this chapter to shift your perspective. This shift can be delicate. As we've discussed, our early spiritual journey is often about identifying and letting go of some of the old beliefs that no longer serve us. A judging God or an exclusive religion might be one such idea. As we grow, we might find our old beliefs to be outdated, even counterproductive. However, if we simply turn around and say, "You're wrong!" to the religion and the beliefs we grew up with or have grown away from, we're only contributing to the habits of judgment: "I'm judging you for being judgmental." This doesn't transport us very far. We've just moved our "rightness" to a different level.

We can practice the principle of non-judgment no matter where we are spiritually (or politically or socially). Because whenever we reach a level of comfort with our ideas and beliefs, there's the temptation to put down roots, to say "At last, I've found the truth." And whenever that happens, the tendency to judge creeps back in. That's why we see terribly judgmental attitudes, statements, and behaviors throughout the spiritual, political and social spectrums. As a species, we are not thoroughly immune from a tendency to judge. At least not yet. But we, as individuals on a spiritual path, do have a choice in moving beyond judgment and toward a more harmonious way of being in the world. As we recognize our own habits of judgment, we will be more likely to question, not judge, our ideas about Spirit, our images of the divine, our notions about society and government and…everything. That move from judgment to questioning is a simple reflection of how we are with ourselves internally, and how we are with others. So, moving beyond judgment in our own lives in turn allows us to enter the realm of presence.

What is Mindfulness?

A lot has been said about presence and mindfulness recently, which illustrates how we are growing in consciousness to a place where more of us are aware of this practice. I'm grateful for this because it's through awareness, through the practice of absolute presence, that we begin to become more awake to how we create what we call reality. Presence is a conscious willingness to be right here in this moment. The reason I'm discussing it here, after nonresistance and non-judgment, is that once we have begun to practice a way of being in the world that is free from judgment and free from resistance, we land in a space that is more peaceful and joy-filled.

Many of us have spent a great deal of time developing all sorts of strategies to not be present, to not live right here in this moment. That's partly because of our approach—most of us have been taught to go through life identifying problems and seeking solutions. This means, essentially, that the current situation is never OK. "If only I could get that promotion, then things will be OK," "If she could just understand me, then things will be better." With this worldview, there's always something out there to strive for. There's always somewhere better than here. Our job, even our purpose, is to control, to improve, to "fix" our circumstances.

This is a focus on the future, on what might be "if only." The flip side of this future focus is looking back on the past. From that perspective, we regret actions we took, or didn't take. Here we might criticize ourselves for failing, not doing the "right" thing, not seeing the problem or finding the solution. So again, we get stuck in patterns of shame and judgment. If we've been living life this way, it can be difficult to wrap our heads around the experience of mindfulness or presence, which is about relating to ourselves right in this moment. We've gone so long without being aware of what's happening in the present that we can't even tell what we're feeling or experiencing right now.

What if presence is our natural state, but we've been programmed to not be in the moment, to be constantly reliving the past or worrying about the future? From this perspective, maintaining presence involves unlearning more than learning. Once we come to the point where the strategy of future/past focus no longer works for us, we can unlearn our un-present way of being. And then we might find that presence isn't that difficult, because it is our essential nature. We do this unlearning in part through mindfulness practice, which includes meditation. Meditation is an incredibly powerful way to practice not only a mindful state during the actual meditation session, but a mindful way of being in the world.

Practicing Mindfulness

As with everything else on this journey, our awareness shapes our experience. And my early experience of meditation was frustrating. As I mentioned earlier, I thought that the goal of meditation was to learn to quiet the mind or empty the mind. For at least a decade, I truly believed that meditation was supposed to bring me to a state of emptiness, a blissful experience of tapping into the divine. So, each time I sat on my meditation pillow I would say, "OK, mind— be quiet." It was aggressive. The more I told my mind to be quiet, the louder it seemed to get. And I couldn't seem to "fix" it.

So, even mindfulness can be approached as something we lack, something we need to fix, to learn. "If only I could learn how to be more present..." Even a search for mindfulness can keep us stuck in patterns of shame, anxiety, and restlessness if it's founded on a core false belief. Fortunately, what I further came to understand is that the fundamental benefit of meditation is it allows us to practice being in awe and in wonder of what's happening right in the moment. Meditation is a way to witness ourselves, to be an observer of ourselves physically, mentally, emotionally, and spiritually, no matter how loud or quiet our thinking is. And by witnessing our thoughts, we can come to understand that they do not represent the totality of "reality."

Our thoughts, emotions, and bodies are not the whole of our experience or our identity. In meditation, we can learn to be observers of our bodies, emotions, and our thoughts. We can simply sit with them and observe what's happening with them. "How tight are my shoulders and neck? What's going on in my stomach? Look at that memory that just floated into my mind. What am I feeling right now?" In this way, our perspective broadens from "I am my body" or "I am my thoughts," to "I have a body" or "I have thoughts." Witnessing creates a space that separates us from our thoughts, emotions and our bodies, and in that process we become freed from the false belief that we *are* those thoughts and ideas. We are simply practicing a different perspective—looking through the eyes of the observer. And yes, this practice can be transformative.

This practice can transform not only the moments during meditation but how we operate in the world after meditation. As we practice the power of mindfulness, our confidence is strengthened, and we have more awareness of what's happening in and around us. Mindfulness allows us to feel more deeply, think more clearly. So yes, if you choose to practice mindfulness you will experience change. Remember, mindfulness as a practice of witnessing allows us to bring absolute clarity to this very moment. When we witness what the thoughts, emotions and our bodies are doing in the moment of meditation, all sorts of things can be revealed. So, we need to be in a place where this revelation is what we want, where we are ready to make that decision to grow in our awareness.

Practicing Witness Consciousness

By witnessing our thoughts, we can recognize our limitations, we can identify places where we might be stuck. For instance, let's say during meditation we think, "This is so hopeless. I should have known I'd be too anxious to get this meditation stuff." If we *are* that thought, if we truly believe that we are too anxious, then chances are we'll get stuck in it. It will look like truth to us, and there's no escaping that. But if instead we *have* that thought, if we witness it from the distance of meditation, then it's not us, it's not truth—it's just a thought. So, rather than being dismayed or depressed by it, we can be curious about it. We can be unstuck; we can be free.

Similarly, by witnessing our thoughts, emotions and bodies, by noticing how we physically and emotionally respond to what's happening during meditation, we can discover all sorts of things. For example, perhaps during meditation you realize that you forgot to send an email before you left the office, and your stomach suddenly lurches and your heart starts pounding. If you have no distance from that physical response, if you believe that your stomach and your heart at that moment are telling the whole truth, then that experience of anxiety will grow in power, and very likely you will only get more anxious the longer you sit there.

But if you witness your stomach and your heart, if you notice what they are doing from a place beyond them, then you'll be able to calm down. Witnessing will allow you to wonder, to look for what's happening. "Interesting. I wonder what lies beneath that feeling in my stomach." Again, it's curiosity, rather than fear or judgment. It can be quite liberating. And, paradoxically, the more you practice witnessing your thoughts, the quieter your mind will become.

The Benefits of Presence

Another powerful practice is to simply commit to engaging with present moment awareness. For example, the next time you are doing the dishes, can you take time to actually feel the dish? Can you really notice the warm water? What smells and sensations can you become aware of? Maybe the next time you are walking, you can bring focus to the way your feet feel as they touch the ground. Noticing your everyday activities with a new and deeper awareness can be a powerful tool in becoming more mindful.

Being present doesn't mean we stop thinking about the future or the past. It doesn't mean we stop preparing or remembering. What being present does is change the quality of our plans and our memories. It helps us to recognize, on the deep level of the feeling tone, that we are not projected there, into the future. We are not stuck there, in the past. We are here, absolutely present. As we learn in meditation to become the observer, then we can expand the practice to our daily lives. We can notice our thought patterns and deeply held perspectives, we can notice when we're sitting in the past or the future instead of the present. As we notice more, we can shift from opinions and worldviews that keep us limited in "rightness" and "wrongness." When we let go of the need to control, to fix, to be "right," we can rest in the moment, surrender our strategies, our opinions, our perspectives. We can have the experience of presence, of connection, of who and what we really are.

So, living in present moment awareness is witnessing all of life from a place of oneness with Source. It is making a commitment to bringing deep attention to this very moment. And that changes everything. Is it possible to be in a state of presence and mindfulness every moment of every day? I say yes. And, at very least, we know it *is* possible to be more and more present each day. Through the practice of presence and mindfulness we can *be* that presence in the world. And, when we are present, we are open to the subtle inner and outer messages that can gently direct our lives in a more positive and grounded direction.

Living in the Question

Living in the question is another very powerful spiritual practice we can use to break free from addiction and live a more connected life. It's a great tool for developing mindfulness, because it trains us to notice what our points of view influence us to see. As I've pointed out before, most of us have been trained from a very young age to solve problems, to "find the answer"—whether that's the answers to life's questions or the answers on a test at school. We might even believe that finding the answers is our purpose in life. Many of us move into a spiritual practice with this same intention. We begin our practice by looking for the answers, thinking that if we can just "figure out the meaning of life" we will be okay.

It's easy to find examples of how people of different religions have lived by this approach over the centuries. By teaching that they have "the answer," that their way is the only way, various religions end up excluding people and ideas and rejecting other ways of doing things. This is a good example of how this approach ends up limiting, rather than expanding our knowledge and our perspective. It's also an example of how conflict gets created. If Christianity finds its answer in the Bible, and Islam finds its answer in the Koran, there might be conflict where those two sources differ. If people in this group believe communism is the answer and people in that group believe capitalism is the answer, then they will have conflict where those approaches differ.

An answer-focused approach can create conflict on a personal level as well. When I believe that I have the answer but you see it another way, that means you don't have the correct answer. I am right and you are wrong, and there's external conflict. Or if I believe that there's an answer out there but I am not able to reach it, or do not deserve to reach it, then there's internal conflict. Almost always, conflict comes from the notion that there is a right and a wrong answer, that someone has the answer and other answers (and thus other people) are wrong. Approaching life as a search for the answer can keep us stuck in the comfort zone of our false core beliefs, our small view of the world which assumes there's only one way, one answer.

As we've seen, it can be difficult to let go of this approach. I certainly thought it was the way to look at things when I first came into spiritual practice. I figured there was a "right" way to believe and act, and if I could just figure it out I would grow spiritually. Then came a beautiful turning point. I don't know if it was an event or a gradual process, but at some point, I began to open to the possibility that it's not about coming up with the answer, it is about living in the question and opening to this great mystery. At some point, I began seeing my purpose not as spiritual growth toward some perfect state, but as growing in awareness of a perfection that already is.

Maybe that's another difference between religion and spirituality. Religion is here to provide the answer; spirituality is here to ask questions. And in my experience, the practice of living in the question is more powerful than that of searching for the answer. An answer-focused approach is steeped in ego; it can't help but be infused with our personal desires because the thing we are trying to change, whatever that may be, depends on the answer.

We need the answer to work for us. So, when we end up finding an answer, it's limited by our personal bias, our core false beliefs, our judgment. Focusing on the question, on the other hand, provides a distance between me (the person asking the question) and the answer (whatever it is that I find). Living in the question allows us to approach things from a position of curiosity rather than anxiety, of play rather than urgency. And that's mindfulness, really. It's non-judgment and nonresistance.

Practicing the Questioning Process

How exactly do we go about living in the question? It's actually quite simple: We ask ourselves open-ended questions that do not start with "Why." These are questions like, "Who else might I want to connect with now?" "What can I do next?" "How can I discover what is mine to do?" "Where else might I look?" These are who, where, what, and how questions. My favorite question currently is "What else is possible?" Being open-ended, these questions cannot be answered with a simple yes or no. They don't claim to have a simple answer. Life is more nuanced than that. With open-ended questions, we are less likely to create answers based on past experiences, and open up to new possibilities. We can open up rather than contract.

We might think of it in terms of science. We can view science as a discipline that shows us facts about the universe, that gives us answers. But the answers that science gives are continually changing as scientists learn more. Ideally, science is endlessly open to ever deeper understanding, and doesn't assume to know an absolute answer. It's more about examining questions. That's what a scientific hypothesis is, really—a "what if" question. So, living in the question is, in a way, like living the scientific method, in an open stance that does not assume that the answers will stand for all time or for all people.

Why no "why" questions? With "why" questions we are tempted to immediately search for the answer. With why questions we're subtly telling ourselves that there's some explanation, and if we can just figure that out, things will shift. Life will change. It's interesting that most of the questions we ask from a victim mentality are "why" questions. "Why is she like that?" "Why are people so stupid?" "Why is this happening to me?" "Why does he treat me like that?" Why questions often assume that we have been wronged. They assume not only that there is a right answer, but that the answer involves our victimization. They close off other possibilities. And if there's only one answer, then there's only one option. This is the kind of thinking that traps us, that limits our freedom. When we live in the question, we're focused not on finding the answer but on opening to the possibilities, finding a way to expand our consciousness to awaken to a broader view of ourselves and the world. It's an expansion of our awareness. When we live in the question our focus is not on change, or improvement, or reaching some ultimate goal. Our focus is on expanding our awareness of what else is possible. Questions expand. Answers contract.

Here are some ideas for starting this practice: You might bring an open-ended question to your meditation practice. Ask the question and pay attention to what you are experiencing physically, mentally, and emotionally. Stay open to the awareness this brings. In another practice, you sit in front of a mirror, or face a partner. Set the clock for three minutes, and then present the question to your reflection in the mirror, or have your partner ask you the question. Over the set time, stay open to whatever awareness comes to you. After each short answer, repeat the question. Another practice is to focus on a question throughout the day. Pick a question the night before, or as soon as you wake up. Then live in that question as you move through your day. For example, if today's question is, "What more is there for me to see?" then throughout the day you will sit with that question. While you are in the shower, while you're waiting for an appointment or are sitting in traffic, while you're preparing dinner, you'll ask yourself the question and see what emerges.

I also invite you to notice if your questions are empowering or dis-empowering. If you observe yourself asking dis-empowering questions, you might want to replace them with questions that open you up to more possibilities, rather than cause you to shut down. For example, if you lose your job, you might find yourself asking questions like, "Why does this keep happening to me?" or "What is wrong with me?" Here are examples of more empowering questions you may ask yourself: "What is wanting to emerge here?" "What might be my opportunity for growth?" or "How can I allow this to move me forward in my life?" Notice how these questions open you up to the infinite possibilities that this situation contains.

In this process, we are allowing our awareness to increase rather than seeking absolute answers. We allow the question to get deep in our consciousness and we wait for possible information. We pay attention to all the places the information might come from. The initial awareness might seem to come from the mind, then from the gut, then from the heart space, and finally from an even deeper place. My hope for you is this: that as you live with the question, possibilities will come to you from a deeper place, from a place of acceptance, wholeness and transformation.

Accepting Impermanence

As we live in the question and expand and shift our awareness to encompass a greater reality, we come to recognize that nothing is permanent in the outer realm. When we make peace with this fundamental truth, we allow ourselves to shift into a way of being in the world that connects with what is permanent, which is Source or love or light-that which we truly are. So, as we open and let go of our normal way of seeing and being, we recognize that there is a deeper level of awareness, and we can live from this greater reality.

We often live under the assumption that things are permanent. "This job is perfect," "This relationship will last," "This book will stand the test of time." This is the sort of underlying assumption that helps us get through life, correct? But we all know deep down that permanence is not real. It's a concept that we lay on the circumstances of our lives in order to pretend, to live in denial of impermanence, of endings, of death. It's a delusion. The problem with this delusion is that it ends up limiting us. Any time we hold onto something as true just because we need it to be true, that attachment, that necessity will trap us into a limited way of living.

When we struggle to grasp onto or control things in the outer realm, we are usually acting from a sense of helplessness about what's happening internally. We don't know how to process what lies in the shadow, so we clutch at permanence, at security, at "stuff." If we need to believe that things last forever, then we won't have the perspective that comes with the longer view. It will feel as if whatever we're experiencing now is all there is, whether that's a depressive episode, a bit of good fortune, or a loss. Fortunately, when we make peace with impermanence in the outer realm we get to connect with what *is* permanent. And once we have made a deep connection with the bedrock of our being, we can recognize that what's happening in the outer realm is far less significant. From this space of Spirit, we get to witness the changing events of life as fleeting on a fundamental level.

Releasing Control

I'm reminded of the Tibetan Buddhists who make beautiful sand mandalas. You may have seen these. They spend many hours meticulously creating a masterpiece out of sand, and the moment it's finished they sweep it all away. That is a meditation practice, it's a practice of making peace with impermanence. Even the most beautiful, the most valuable things in the universe are impermanent. This doesn't mean they're not beautiful. It just means they're impermanent. And it's clinging *to* and averting *from* these impermanent things that causes suffering. We can make peace with impermanence, first, by allowing what's transpiring in the outer realm to come and go, recognizing that in the realm of Spirit it does not affect us and, second, by developing a practice of connecting with what is changeless and eternal. Connecting with our essential nature, cultivating a profound relationship with that essential part of ourselves that doesn't change, is the greatest way for us to make peace with impermanence.

Imagine you're at a beach and you're going to build a sand castle. You know the sand castle will be washed away by the tide. And yet you build the sand castle anyway, just for the experience of building the sand castle.

What happens in our outer realm is like that sand castle. Everything we are building, everything we're creating, everything we are doing, loving, and experiencing in our outer realm will one day get washed away. Making peace with that certainly doesn't mean we stop interacting or loving or being deeply passionate. On the contrary—when we shift our awareness it ultimately creates more joy, more presence, and more excitement about our lives.

When we are trying to control a certain outcome, when we need things to stay a certain way, we miss the opportunity for happiness. Making peace with impermanence is a way that we can live in the world with awe and wonder and creativity and yet be at peace with what happens in the cycles of life. Clinging to permanence causes suffering, embracing impermanence allows us to open up to joy.

PART 3

A RETURN TO WHOLENESS

Breaking the cycle of addiction by creating safe places in which to unlearn our core false beliefs and to foster our conscious awareness leaves us free to experience a transformed life. What does that life look like? Who are we once we are freed from a belief in our own brokenness and victimization?

Where can we go once we're no longer tied to those limited and limiting stories about who and what we are? What impact does our authenticity have on our outlook, our relationships, our communities? How do we move into a life of more awe and wonder, filled with present-moment awareness, true freedom and purpose?

The chapters in Part 3 of this book describe the potential that lies before you as you go deeper into the room of Spirit. Chapter 7 will explore how you can tap into and own a deeper sense of conscious awareness and will provide methods for moving your life from powerless to power-full. In Chapter 8 we will uncover the divine movement you can experience as you emerge from the cycle of addiction: from letting go to welcoming the shifts in your life, welcoming love and connection, and finally, experiencing divine integration. Finally, Chapter 9 investigates what it means to find a deep sense of purpose and a life filled with peace and happiness—this life of the new paradigm.

Much of what is covered in this section can have multiple meanings, depending on your level of conscious awareness. So, it's important to have done some of the work described in Part 2 before digging into this section.

Chapter Seven

OWNING YOUR POWER

Our deepest fear is not that we are inadequate. Our deepest fear is that we are powerful beyond measure. It is our light, not our darkness that most frightens us. We ask ourselves, who am I to be brilliant, gorgeous, talented, fabulous? Actually, who are you not to be? You are a child of God. Your playing small does not serve the world. There is nothing enlightened about shrinking so that other people won't feel insecure around you. We are all meant to shine, as children do. We were born to make manifest the glory of God that is within us. It's not just in some of us; it's in everyone. And as we let our own light shine, we unconsciously give other people permission to do the same. As we are liberated from our own fear, our presence automatically liberates others.

—Marianne Williamson, A Return to Love

There's a lot of talk in recovery circles about admitting your powerlessness, and early in recovery it can be imperative to acknowledge that your addictive behavior and your unconscious reactions are running the show, so to speak. But as you grow in spiritual awareness, your perspective will shift. You'll return to the limitless possibilities of life, and to a sense of your oneness with Source, the ultimate power. As you focus on your inner work and develop more conscious awareness, you will move from being powerless to being a vessel *for* power, to being one *with* power.

In this chapter, I'm inviting you to consider how you can move from powerlessness to feeling empowered, and discovering your *true* power. This power is different from *will* power, different from *force* or coercion; it's not "making things happen." It's tapping into the ultimate truth of who and what you are. As you grow in conscious awareness and begin to recognize that your core beliefs are really choices, as you find and participate in supportive communities where you feel safe enough to be vulnerable, to be authentic, as you begin to consciously choose to practice the principles of non-resistance, non-judgment, presence, and so on, you can begin to experience the power of who and what you truly are. Specifically, there are five aspects of power I would like to examine here: the power of perception, the power of forgiveness, the power of compassion, the power of authenticity, and the power of gratitude.

The Power of Perception

All spiritual power is based on a shift in perception, and the fundamental insight that ultimate reality, the invisible, is more powerful than relative, or visible, reality. As we grow in awareness, we develop the ability to shift how we interpret the circumstances of life and what we call reality. Our powers of perception get clearer. How much of life is perception? All of it. We each see the world through our own lens. Multiple people in the same situation will each have a different experience of it, based on the lens through which they see it. It's not that one person sees the truth and the others are wrong. It's that our perception colors our experience.

As our understanding of this increases, our suffering diminishes. If we live as if there is a reality out there, a truth that's external to our perception, if we're holding on to the idea that things are happening *to* us, we will suffer. Suffering comes from living in duality, in the idea of a separate self, in a belief in "us" and "everyone and everything else." From this perspective, we continue to plant the seeds of separation.

When I first shifted to the possibility that all of life is perception, I began to ask myself questions about what I was seeing and experiencing rather than having an opinion about it or a judgment of it. I began to ask distinctive questions. Instead of, "Why is life this way?" I asked, "What if I *looked* at life another way?" This shift, from believing that reality is what I see to knowing it can be experienced differently, is a point of incredible power, because as we begin to see that different perspectives are possible, we become more aware of our choices, and thus our power. So, the power of perception is simply this capacity to recognize that there is an endless variety of lenses through which we can view the world. And it's also the ability to change our perspective, to play with different lenses and see what happens to our experience of what we call reality. It's the ability to choose a perspective that's more open to love and connection.

Here's a simple way to view this: Let's say it's 75 degrees and sunny outside. Many people will experience that as "good weather," as "a beautiful day." Conversely, we tend to judge cold and wet weather as "bad weather" or "a miserable day." What happens when we shift our perception and see sun and rain as equally suitable? A sleet storm and a cloudless sky as equally beautiful? From that modification in perception, our experience also shifts. Rather than fighting against the rain, we could appreciate its moisture. Rather than complaining about the cold, we could feel the bite, welcome the iciness, and see what is there for us to experience. In that way, we can empower ourselves to create a life filled with awe and curiosity, regardless of outer circumstances.

There is an incredible story that illustrates the power of perspective beautifully. A neuroscientist was studying a group of people who were born blind, and were later given corrective surgery that allowed them to see. The assumption was that once the surgery was complete, they would be able to see everything in their environment perfectly. However, to their surprise, it actually took hours, days, or even weeks for them to have *full* restoration of their eyesight. What's more, they discovered that people could only immediately see what they already understood or had experienced. In other words, they could only see what they already knew to be "true."

In one case, someone held an apple in their hand and showed it to someone who had just had the corrective surgery. The person could see the hand but not the apple! Only over a bit of time, could they begin to see that apple. As they continued the study, they discovered that the brain literally only sees what we *already* hold as a concept. We can easily see how this creates limitation based on our deeply held concepts and ideas about ourselves and the world. *We have power to shift our perception and therefore shift how we experience life.*

Shifting Perception

Here's a review of a concept we covered in an earlier chapter: Pain and suffering are two different things. Pain is in the body; suffering is in the mind. Pain, at least at our current stage of evolution, seems to be an inevitable part of the human experience. Suffering, on the other hand, is usually based on the belief that something should be different than what it is. Suffering happens when we resist pain, when we come up with strategies to avoid, numb, or forget pain. It occurs when we isolate ourselves in our pain. This suffering is at the root of addiction, because addiction happens when we're trying to find something outside of ourselves to end or numb our pain.

When we greet the pain, when we experience it and allow it to move *through* us, we end suffering. That may seem counterintuitive, but my invitation to you is to ask yourself: What is the difference between pain and suffering in your experience? And is it possible that you can feel the pain without moving into suffering? As you let go of your core false beliefs and move beyond your limited and limiting stories, can you feel the power of this shift in perception? Where is it leading you today? How are you responding to this experience of openness?

As I hope you are finding, when we let go of our self-limiting beliefs and expand in our awareness to move into wholeness, things look different and so things *are* different. Look at Oprah Winfrey. You might think that as a black woman who had endured sexual abuse, she would experience life as limited and limiting. Instead, her life has been an example of abundance and limitlessness. How did this happen? She decided to live beyond her programming, to open to a life filled with possibility, rather than staying stuck in the "reality" that was modeled to her. Let me say it again: *When we let go of our self-limiting beliefs and expand our awareness, things look different and so they become different.* We move into power.

The Power of Forgiveness

Forgiveness is a very powerful tool in letting go of the perspectives that keep us in a limited and limiting way of seeing and being. Forgiveness allows us to move more deeply into the truth of who and what we are, to eradicate our stories of separation, powerlessness, and being stuck in blaming and victimization. Many of us have a terrifically hard time with forgiveness. We feel that terrible things have happened in our lives, and we are unable to let them go. So, let's start there, with the experience of forgiveness that many of us have had. When we're stuck in unconscious reactions, forgiveness is next to impossible. The beliefs we hold about ourselves and our world become the lens through which we view the world, the way we frame our stories. They limit our perspective and block us from freedom and authenticity. When we're living at this victim/martyr level of consciousness, hearing about the need to forgive can push us further into limitation.

If we are holding the idea that we're fundamentally a victim, then "forgiveness" may look like admitting that we are "wrong" or "bad," that we "deserve what we get." Or it can look like giving up, admitting that the other person is stronger or better and that we cannot ever win. From this level of awareness, forgiveness supposes that we've been harmed, or have lost, and that we need to forgive the person who harmed us, which can feel like basically admitting that the person who hurt us has won. From the perspective of a victim, forgiveness might also mean pretending that things that happened in the past never happened. This requires forgetting, and burying things deep in the shadow.

Either way, this kind of forgiveness can further strengthen the belief in our own victimization because it's based on the idea that something "bad" needs to be made right by either rationalizing it or burying it. This tends to create more suffering, more limitation. And that is not empowerment. As you begin to identify and let go of all those deeply held beliefs about yourself and the world that keep you in a reactive state, as you experience more authenticity in the safety of supportive community, as you practice the spiritual principles described in chapter 6, as you open to the power of Spirit, your experience of forgiveness will begin to shift.

Deepening Forgiveness

We may think of forgiveness as making peace with the past. That means different things from different perspectives. From a place of non-judgment, the past is what it is. The past cannot be different— we cannot go back and change what happened. But we can alter the way we see it. As the saying goes, *"It's never too late to have a happy childhood."* What this quote means to me is that as we do our healing work, we can look at the past through a different lens. We can truly find a place of gratitude no matter how our childhood looked. This is in no way saying that we don't sometimes feel pain or sadness about our past. What it is pointing to is that we have the power within ourselves to reframe and find gratitude in *any* of our past situations.

This shift may not happen overnight, and in certain situations reconciliation might not be easy. Even as you're doing the internal work and growing in awareness, you may still tend to experience forgiveness as directed outward, focusing on how someone, even you, has treated others rather than on your own inner movement. If your experience of forgiveness pushes you back into your stories of victimhood, that may mean you need to do some more of the work described in earlier chapters to help break the cycle. Or it may just mean you need to ask yourself some further questions, to reap the benefits of all the inner work you've been doing. So, let's look at some of those questions.

Think of a situation in which you find it difficult to forgive. What is the story you have been telling about that situation? Where have you been especially attached to that story—what belief does it support? Is there another way to look at it? Keeping that situation in mind, what happens when you let go of the idea that one story is "right?" What happens when you approach what happened with the neutrality of an impartial observer? Can you let go of your initial reactive story about the situation and open yourself to other possible perspectives? If you can, what happens when you do that?

Forgiveness and Accountability

When we let go of the ego's attachment to a particular story or a specific verdict about who is "right" and who is "wrong," could it be that we no longer even *need* to forgive? If we release our hold on "right" or "wrong," it's easier to see people as reacting and responding out of their own perspectives, their own limited experiences and imperfect knowledge. It's then a relatively short step to move from guilt, remorse, and forgiveness to something more like responsibility, resolution, and reconciliation. We don't need to ignore the pain in our lives. For instance, we would not stay in an abusive relationship out of the idea that "There is no guilt here; whatever happens, happens." We would not believe that we are no longer accountable for our actions because, "Hey, I've let go of ego." That is not witness consciousness. It's possibly denial.

Of course, we're accountable. Of course, we might still feel pain. When we feel hurt, our first reaction might be to feel anger, to lash out, to want to harbor a grudge. When we experience those reactions in conscious awareness, we might still feel that pain, but then we go on to witness it, to observe our reactions, and then choose how to respond, letting go of the need for someone to be wrong or right. Similarly, if we do something that causes pain to someone else, we may still feel an initial trigger of shame, and maybe from that feeling springs defensive anger. In conscious awareness, we're able to look at these reactions compassionately, which empowers us to then move beyond them to choose the next step.

When we arrive at the mystical level of consciousness, of recognizing our oneness with life, there is no longer anything to forgive. This place of alignment with ultimate reality acknowledges that the cause of anyone's harmful behavior is separation from their essential self. When we reach a state of oneness with Source through the process we've been examining throughout this book, we recognize that *there's nothing to forgive because we can see that everything that's happened in our life has played a part in our transformation; it's been useful in getting us where we are.* And as we grow in conscious awareness, forgiveness becomes more of a natural process. At this level of awareness, we shift from forgiveness to compassion and gratitude.

The Power of Compassion

Much of my work involves sitting with clients as they describe their pain and their suffering. I used to think that my job as a compassionate counselor was to identify in their stories what was "wrong," and then help them fix it. As I did my own work of inner healing, I began to understand that compassion isn't about judging what's wrong and helping to fix it, it's about being one with the other and seeing our shared humanity. Pema Chödrön puts it this way: *"Compassion is not a relationship between the healer and the wounded. It's a relationship between equals. Only when we know our own darkness well can we be present with the darkness of others. Compassion becomes real when we recognize our shared humanity."* When I am willing to see beyond the story, beyond the behavior, and beyond the symptoms, something profound transpires. When I witness clients as whole and perfect, something profound transpires. When I hold a space for them to access their own inner wisdom, something profound transpires. As Rachel Naomi Remen writes, *"We do not serve the weak or the broken. What we serve is the wholeness of each other and the wholeness in life."*

My first spiritual teacher, Mary Helen Brownell, once led a group of us on a pilgrimage to India. Our first stop, and the journey's first lesson, was at LAX, where we waited for many hours. In the waiting area was a young mother who was becoming very frustrated with her infant and scolding loudly. Soon I could feel the judgment in the room as people became angry with the mother. Mary Helen diffused that tension quite simply. She walked calmly up to the woman and said kindly, "I was a young mother once, and I know how frustrating it can be. How can I help you?" She sat with this young woman for about half an hour. I didn't hear anything else that was said in this interlude, but Mary Helen's simple action had a profound impact on me. It showed me that we can either judge or we can serve. We can either judge or we can love. We have a choice in how we respond to life.

Some of us have difficulty imagining how this level of compassion is possible even when faced with something fairly minor like someone who is annoying us, a crying baby, or an unhelpful airline representative during a long flight delay. A deeper question beyond that is, how can I respond with compassion in the face of a seemingly unbearable injustice or intense pain? Yes, even then it's possible. When such an event happens in our own lives—or in the world, as it does so often—the first step is to feel whatever we're feeling as deeply as possible, and to honor whatever time this process takes.

Feeling Your Feelings

If you experience pain, then let that happen. Really allow yourself to feel whatever feelings are present. When you allow yourself to actually feel the emotions, they organically move through you rather than getting trapped or buried. When it comes to emotions, the only way out is through. Practicing this allows you to feel great sorrow and loss, even anger, while also feeling compassion. It also allows the natural, impermanent process of the feeling to dissipate after you give yourself permission to be fully present with whatever shows up.

Remember, feeling your feelings and responding in a conscious way is distinctly different than having a feeling and *reacting* to it. If you react to any situation without tapping into conscious awareness, you are simply continuing what caused the situation in the first place. Say you perceive that someone in your life has been treated unfairly. In response to that experience you might feel angry, and in turn you might want to figure out who is to blame, even to seek revenge. If you *react* from feelings without questioning them, if you actively identify "the person who did this" as the problem, if you actively judge or hurt the person, it only adds to the aggression that created the original situation. You are only continuing the cycle of violence.

Feelings are present for a reason. They are the internal navigation system that is letting us know something needs attention. The issue for many of us is that we believe a person or a situation "make us" feel a certain way. When we become fully accountable for our emotions, we can begin to dialog and question the deeper root causes of our feelings. Are they coming from a story or an old idea we are holding? Is there another way to view the situation? The key here is accountability. When we take ownership for our emotional response (or reaction) to a situation, we recognize it is not the situation that causes us to feel a certain way. It is quite possibly an unhealed wound that has been touched, and with this awareness, we can find freedom in the midst of any emotional experience. In this way, we can begin to shift the feeling itself.

As a conscious being, your feelings of anger or frustration or vengefulness may still emerge. However, as you allow yourself to feel the emotions and practice witness consciousness, you will not be imprisoned by them. They won't force you to *react* in anger. If you have feelings of anger, you can choose to feel the feelings deeply, allow them to pass through you, then respond in love and acceptance. And the more you do this, the easier it becomes. Over time, you will discover that feelings, like anger, subside the more you practice this.

The Power of Authenticity

How many times have you felt obligated to respond positively when someone says, "Hi, how are you?" Many of us answer "Great!" or "Blessed!" or "Awesome!" even when we're not feeling any of those things. That's a *surface* example of what many of us feel internally: that what's important is to look good on the outside, to hide our suffering. We sometimes feel it's an act of weakness to be honest and talk about what's truly happening. This kind of inauthenticity is at the root of addiction. The strategies we use for hiding, for keeping secrets, for avoiding honesty, can lead to addictive behaviors. One of the root causes of addiction, as we saw in Part 1, is toxic shame, and shame needs inauthenticity to survive. It needs secrecy and silence. The addiction that inauthenticity creates can create chaos in your life and the lives of others, and it can even kill you. As Brené Brown stated in her groundbreaking book, *The Gifts of Imperfection*: *"Authenticity is a collection of choices that we have to make every day. It's about the choice to show up and be real. The choice to be honest. The choice to let our true selves be seen."*

Even when we're coming out of addiction, often we're still hiding, we're not ready to be wholly ourselves, to honor the full range of who and what we are with others, or even with ourselves. Many people I work with who are entering recovery will say things like, "If you really knew me, you could not possibly love me." That's toxic shame, which can lead to separation and can create the cycle of addiction. On a spiritual level, though, recovery calls us to be authentic, to bring our whole self into the room. We experience a deeper healing when we're not so caught up in the fear of "looking bad" or in the desire to "look good."

In conscious recovery, it's not about eradicating what we consider "bad" or "negative," it's about embracing it, allowing it to be, and recognizing that it is not the ultimate truth of who and what we are. As we grow in safe supportive community, we feel able to be more authentic, and we find more ways to fully integrate. We can experience this in any recovery program where there is encouragement, and any community that shows us how to be more vulnerable and authentic. Through conscious community we can create relationships and spaces in our lives where we can be more of who we truly are, where we can speak our truth *even when our voice breaks.*

Embracing Authentic Wholeness

In the realm of ultimate reality, nothing is essentially broken. When we can live from this truth, the process of recognizing those parts of ourselves that feel broken and bringing them to the light so that they can get healed is deeper and more profound. It's by working through our dark periods, by uncovering our deepest shames and sorrows, that we can have our greatest transformation—if that courageous authenticity is rooted in the truth of who and what we are. The power of authenticity becomes evident when we witness our darkness from a place of wholeness and perfection.

Remember the discussion about attachment styles in an earlier chapter? Well, authenticity plays a major role in moving us into healthy attachment, because having the courage to be our fully authentic self and speak about what is truly happening for us is a way to develop and cultivate healthy and secure attachments in our relationships. I am not referring to "needing" to have our voice, or "speaking our truth" from a victim perspective, although this may be an important stage in our development. I am talking about creating relationships where it is safe to truly share the deeper, more authentic aspects of what we are experiencing.

This also shows up in the communication style we use. Most of you are probably aware of the four communication styles: aggressive, passive, passive-aggressive, and assertive, right? Well, I have reframed the assertive style, and now refer to it as the authentic style of communication. Our communication styles often develop from our family systems, and we have come to use a particular communication style as a strategy to feel safe. Moving toward an authentic communication style allows us to not only feel more comfortable in our own skin, it allows us to have deeper, more meaningful relationships.

There's an additional bonus too: Authenticity grows and is shared. When we have found a safe place to bring *all* of ourselves into the room, including things we have felt shame about and feelings and experiences that lie in the shadow, ultimately we experience more connection, stronger relationships, and a more fully grounded sense of self. As it turns out, people generally respond positively to authenticity. When we can share our experiences of suffering and brokenness, others quite often respond with their own experiences. When we can *really* be ourselves, without worrying about how it looks or seems, that joy is palpable and contagious. That's the power of authenticity. As with all of these gifts, what we feed will grow. As we go deeper into recovery and conscious awareness, we develop more courage to let others truly see us. It gets easier; it becomes our way of being. As a teacher once told me, "The spiritual journey is not about "getting good;" it's about becoming more and more *real*." That's authenticity.

The Power of Gratitude

Gratitude may be one of the most talked-about spiritual principles there is, and many of us have learned that gratitude is a powerful tool for spiritual awakening and recovery. Many of us make gratitude lists, or keep a gratitude journal. This is wonderful. It teaches us to *feel* grateful, to be more open to positivity. That's very important for those of us working to let go of the emotional habits left over from our core false beliefs. If we're working on unlearning, if we're letting go of our stories of victimization, if we're trying to stop living as if the world is doing something *to* us, then we can strengthen our gratitude by finding something to be grateful for in *every* situation, finding whatever light appears in the midst of the darkness. For there is always light.

From that insight, I want to take things a little deeper by talking about the tendency to *force* gratitude. Sometimes it seems like "living in gratitude" means we need to feel *perpetually* grateful. Our desire to be grateful might lead us to believe that we need to feel love for and harmony with everything and everyone, 24-7. Some spiritual communities, for example, seem to want to focus only on the light, to call everything good without addressing the deeper shadow, or the darkness. When we talk only about love and light without also addressing some of the more difficult experiences we have, it only adds to that familiar pressure to always *pretend* to be happy, which can be inauthentic. And it isn't authentic to force feelings that aren't truly there.

This brings us back to the power of authenticity. What would it be like to be grateful for all aspects of ourselves—not just those things that look like love and light but also the aspects of our shadow? Those things are part of our experience. It's all fuel for transformation. Those parts of ourselves that we would like to change or shift can be helped by holding a space of gratitude, rather than trying to bury them. The more we can be grateful for it *all*, the less blocked we are by shame and blame. This in turn fuels our authenticity. When we are grateful for all experiences, all aspects of ourselves, not just for those things that seem "good," then we have more courage to let others see all of us, which in turn invites more love and connection and more opportunities to rectify those things that need healing. So, gratitude feeds authenticity and authenticity feeds gratitude, in ever-widening circles of love and connection.

It's great to be able to feel gratitude for the "good" things even in the midst of a terrible situation—the community that came together to support those hurt in a hurricane or the policy changes that occurred after a terrible injustice. However, the limit to this approach is that it still categorizes everything: "This was bad, but I'm going to find the good." As soon as we have a feeling of wrongness, of judging the perceived perpetrator, or identifying the heroes in the situation, immediately that judgment solidifies the idea that we are separate. So even our practice of gratitude can end up strengthening duality, judgment, and inauthenticity, rather than focusing on oneness.

Being Gratitude

Our growing awareness can help us when we fall into this pattern. If you become aware that your practice of gratitude is limited and limiting in this way, it may be time to move into a deeper practice: not just being grateful *for* things, not just *feeling* gratitude, but *becoming* gratitude. At this level, gratitude is not only a feeling— it's also a way of seeing and of being. It's a state of gratitude not only *for* the world, but *in* the world. When we're in the midst of a difficult situation, *being* gratitude means honoring the difficulty, acknowledging the feelings of anger, sadness, or frustration, and yet at the same time tapping into the ultimate truth of who and what we are and living from an ultimate allowance of what is. To *be* gratitude, we don't need anything to change in the outer realm.

Nor do we need to change our experience of difficulty or to shut down our feelings.

As our inner vibration of gratitude grows, it manifests more in the outer world, which matches our inner vibration and gives us more and more things to be grateful for. In other words, the more we practice gratitude, the more life seems to give us to be grateful *for*. Even when things we desire have not manifested yet, we can be grateful for their approach, for their transpiring. And this gratitude changes our perspective and thus changes reality.

Another aspect of the power of gratitude lies in our awareness of ultimate truth, which we have been discussing throughout this book. When we can know, and have a feeling tone of our oneness with Spirit, then we can be grateful not only for the things that we see, but also for the healing that we know and trust is happening all around the world. So, I invite you to open to the possibility that you can live in a space of open-hearted awareness and *be* gratitude in the world. Living this way will free you from the need to reject any situation, person, or memory; it allows you to stand in the midst of anything happening and welcome it all.

In some situations, this might mean "finding the good in all of life," or it might mean tapping into that ultimate truth and living from ultimate acceptance of what is. It's a continuous process. In order to *be* gratitude, we continually check back in with our oneness with Source. It's a moment by moment choice. Whenever we recognize that we're judging, whenever we recognize that we're looking at a situation or a person or ourselves with criticism rather than openness, we can choose to return to this connection, which is love and gratitude. In the same way that love and fear cannot possibly live in the same moment, judgment and gratitude can also not co-exist. Whenever we step into judgment, we've stepped out of gratitude. And, each time this happens we can choose to return to the more powerful awareness of gratitude.

I invite you to ask yourself the questions: "What is my experience of gratitude? And is it possible that I can *be* gratitude in the world, in addition to finding things to be grateful *for?*" "Can I choose to return, moment by moment, to my oneness with Spirit?" This is a new way of being and seeing, a transformational power that can alter everything in your life. I invite you to give it a try. After all, life is a great experiment. Why not try it and see what happens?

Chapter Eight

THE GREAT REMEMBERING

> *What all of us most want is the experience of our own essential nature. This yearning is behind every worldly desire. When we are out of contact with our own essence, we look for fulfillment from the world. To fulfill our desires, we develop a strategy that requires repressing some aspect of ourselves because that quality appears to be the threat to the fulfillment of our desires.*
> — *Robert Brumet*, Birthing a Greater Reality

We often live as if our enlightenment is going to happen someday. We treat our spiritual journey like it's a goal we are headed toward, or something we lack and need to attain. We view the spiritual journey through the lens of being broken and needing to be fixed. But as we've seen in this book, we are born into the world already knowing our essential self. So, enlightenment is already present. This means that our spiritual journey is simply a matter of *remembering* this fundamental knowledge, which we may have lost through abandonment, through "the domestication of the human," through unresolved trauma, spiritual disconnection, and toxic shame. This Great Remembering is the source of incredible power: the power to experience great change, the power to embrace love and deepen connection, the power to integrate with our authentic self. This all starts with the process I hope you're experiencing as you work through this book: letting go.

Letting Go

The strategies of resistance and control that we've learned and practiced throughout our lives can leave us feeling trapped in limited and limiting patterns and stories. These strategies keep us frozen in the emotionally triggering charge associated with everything in relative reality, unable to experience life in a fully present way. Stuck in the stories we tell ourselves about "reality," we miss out on what living genuinely is, which is the experience of wonder and awe right here in this moment. To break free of these patterns and stories, we unlearn—we uncover our core false beliefs and integrate what we have hidden in shadow. And in so doing, we let go of the idea of a limited self, a self that is separate from Source. We let go of all our thought patterns, all our beliefs, all those behaviors that keep us small and separate. And in letting go, we come into the experience of *The Great Remembering*: The deeply felt knowing that we are one with Source. We have returned to our state of original perfection.

This kind of letting go is a powerful component of spiritual awakening. There's more power in letting go, in yielding, and in redirecting energy than there is in resisting, controlling, and pushing back. When we're struggling with addiction, we're resisting. We're pushing back against our inner need to be present with ourselves in the moment. Addictive behavior is simply that—a resistance to presence, a strategy for avoiding what's here now because it's too painful or too shameful. Letting go in the context of addiction means not only releasing the idea that we are inherently broken and need to change, but also releasing all the strategies we've perfected for protecting what we perceive as our brokenness. The ultimate surrender is not surrendering those parts of us that are "bad," but surrendering to who and what we are as whole and perfect. This is not about looking perfect on the outside; it's about resting in that original perfection, the blueprint that we are as spiritual beings.

One of the beliefs that many of us are unlearning is that life is about identifying problems and figuring out how to fix them. Letting go opens a major shift in that paradigm; as we let go of the idea that life is a series of problems, we can choose to see that the only problem that exists is a problem we hold in our minds. The only thing that keeps us from waking up to the truth of who and what we are is the idea that we *can't* wake up. The only thing that blocks us from enlightenment is the idea that we are blocked from enlightenment. For some people, this shift comes in an instant. For many of us, it's a lifelong practice of questioning, unlearning, and growing in awareness of our deeper selves.

Making U-Turns

Have you ever realized that it's time for a U-turn? Time to make a radical change in your life? Sometimes we find ourselves going in a direction in which we're not content. When we recognize this, we generally make small adjustments in direction or maneuver slightly to change our trajectory. Most of the changes we make are small because we're more comfortable with what's familiar, and we don't want to move too far into unfamiliar territory.

These small shifts can be valuable. Maybe we're wanting more time for meditation, so we start getting up twenty minutes earlier. This gives us what we want without making a huge disruption in our lives. But occasionally we're ready for a bigger, more significant shift. This is what I'm calling a U-turn. It's not a subtle shift; it's taking life in a distinctively different direction. Maybe we're in a dead-end job or in an unhappy relationship, or we're coming up against the limits of our addictive behavior. Whatever the circumstances, a U-turn is that moment not only of clarity but of courage and willingness to make a major change.

Those of us who have lived with addiction are familiar with the U-turn. For many of us it's mandatory; our recovery will not work if we take only small and subtle turns. We need to turn it around completely. And we know that making the U-turn can be a process. It starts with the awareness that the change is necessary, but it doesn't end there. The change won't happen if all we have is the awareness. We also need the courage and the willingness to make the modification. And as we enter the change, we find that it is manifest in different ways in various areas of our lives.

Often we start our U-turns in the physical room: detoxing from a drug we're addicted to, moving out of a precarious living situation, staying away from our drinking buddies—these are U-turns in the outer realm. These U-turns require us to name the addiction as a problem and admit that we need help. But if we don't move through the other rooms—mental, emotional, and spiritual—chances are we won't permanently break the cycle of addiction. We may change a particular addictive behavior, but our outer-focused search for relief will continue, landing over and over again on other strategies for avoiding or numbing our inner suffering.

The only way to permanently break free from addiction is to have a U-turn in consciousness, a dramatic shift in the way we *relate* to our innermost self. In other words, we break the cycle of addiction by bringing our unconscious thoughts and patterns into conscious awareness, by identifying our core false beliefs and uncovering the root causes of our addiction. This allows us to start seeing addictive behavior as a chosen strategy rather than a problem to be solved. Then we can look more deeply at what we were truly seeking in that strategy, which is most likely love and connection. When we know inwardly—that is, when we truly know and experience that we are not our stories, beliefs, thoughts, emotions, or bodies, but are one with Source—that's the ultimate U-turn. It's a U-turn in consciousness that's not about *doing*, but about *being*. In this ultimate U-turn that breaks the cycle, we turn from an outer-focused way of life to an inner-focused way of being. And as we shift to an inner-focused way of being, the world seems to literally change. It can change in an instant. Those quantum moments, in which we have a dramatic shift in consciousness and recognize that we're not who we always thought we were, allow us to tap into ultimate reality.

U-Turns in Consciousness

There are a couple of potential challenges here: One, how do we create a space for the U-turn in consciousness? And two, what do we need to dismantle and unlearn? What's preventing us from cultivating a relationship with our inner knowing, or from recognizing it for what it is? How can we become more open to all the U-turns in our lives? We clear space for the U-turn in consciousness by doing the inner work. All the shifts and movements described in Part 2 of this book are preparation for a quantum U-turn in your life.

Creating safety, unlearning, practicing spiritual principles, owning your power—as you experience these, I hope you are experiencing greater clarity, as well as courage and willingness, about the endless possibilities that exist in every moment. You may very well be standing on the precipice of a great transformation in your life. As you cultivate a relationship with your essential self, as you become more present and more authentic, you're creating a space for that inner knowing and becoming more open and more receptive to the experience of a shift in consciousness.

In the beginning, it can be challenging to distinguish the vision of our essential self from other, less authentic stories and beliefs. After all, it's often called "the still, small voice" (that deep inner knowing) for a reason. If the negative self-talk and the core false beliefs are still present, they will threaten to drown out the voice that nudges us toward a U-turn, the voice that asks "What if ...?" If we're living from our egos, that voice will remain still and small, hard to distinguish from all the noise in our heads. But that voice doesn't need to be still or small. As we develop, and we are willing to say yes to it and listen, it can become the primary voice. The more we practice our spiritual principles, the clearer and more significant that voice becomes.

The more we are willing to spend time in silent reflection, the more we will learn to hear it, and trust its guidance. So, as we become more practiced, as we more fully live in the new perspective offered by the conscious U-turn, the easier it gets to recognize and move into any U-turn, any new vision for our life. What's exciting is that when when we are still, we might "catch a vision" for our life that comes from Spirit, from our essential self, and it's quite often bigger than what our ego mind would have created or comprehended. That's the power of the conscious U-turn. These visions for our life can happen even when things are going well. Sometimes life is going in a genuinely beautiful direction, and yet if we're spiritually present and authentic, we can hear something inside, the little nudge that says, "What about this?"

That openness manifests in the outer world as well. When you've undergone that quantum shift in consciousness, then you'll be more apt to experience and recognize those serendipitous "coincidences"—when things just seem to work out, when connections are made for "no apparent reason." You will be more in-tune with and aware of the natural rhythm of life. As you experience this more, it will become clear that it's not only a matter of hearing the inner voice; it's also a matter of trusting it to lead you in the outer realm of existence as well.

Imagine a permanent shift in your neural network, in which you don't constantly identify yourself as broken or addicted. Imagine going into a place that used to be filled with triggers, a place that formerly would have looked like a temptation or a trap, and walking through it with ease and grace. Imagine your life as free of "the problem of addiction" and as filled with potential. Imagine that you are truly free to move in whatever direction your inner knowing points. That's the power of the quantum leap, the U-turn in consciousness. Imagine now that, because you are recognizing your oneness with Source, you can absolutely trust its direction. That's the promise of many spiritual practices—that through openness and acceptance, you will develop an unshakable relationship with your inner life, and allow it to gently guide you.

Embracing Love

When I first came to spiritual teachings I was quite young. I had just come out of an addiction and my unconscious was running the show, starting with an unconscious core belief that I was unlovable. Like you, perhaps, I started believing this when I was a child, convinced through a series of events that there was something fundamentally wrong with me. That was one of the root causes of my addiction. Although I was aware that I wanted to break free of the cycle of my addictive behavior, I hadn't yet uncovered its roots. I knew that I was searching for love and connection, but I didn't know that underneath my search was a core false belief that *blocked* love and connection. On the conscious level, I was trying to get people to love me—while on the unconscious level, the belief that I was unlovable was pushing away anything that was authentic love. I was doing the opposite of embracing love.

As my experience shows, when we feel that we're not worthy of love, we will potentially sabotage it when it shows up. That's partly because of what we believe, because we need our experience to resonate with our core false belief in our own unworthiness. But it's also because of how we're *being* in the world. Think about it in terms of energy: Experts tell us that only 10 percent of what we communicate is verbal; the rest is nonverbal. Part of that nonverbal communication is energy. It's the frequency at which we're vibrating, the energy that we're holding. That's what creates what we call reality. We are literally creating what we see and experience in the physical realm based on the vibration we are holding. We're like a radio: You can't hear the radio station until you're tuned into its frequency. So, if we're vibrating at a frequency that says "I'm not lovable," we will tend to attract and be attracted *to* people who can tune into that frequency, people who will verify that core false belief in our own unworthiness.

If we witnessed or experienced a lot of abuse as a child, we're going to quite possibly replicate those abusive relationships unconsciously as adults. I'm not suggesting that we do this consciously—we most likely don't set out to enter an abusive relationship. But unconsciously, our energy will attract those relationships. We will also be open to relationships and situations in which we receive messages that echo our negative inner self-talk—they will feel familiar to us—and we will tend to reject or block out any messages that tell us that we are lovable, that we are a perfect expression of Source. So, embracing love requires a shift in focus, which can be a very subtle, even simple thing. Embracing love is not about trying to force love, or create love, or discover love; it's not about changing how you appear so that people will love you. It's about embracing the love that already is, in others and in yourself. It's knowing and feeling and living the truth that you are made in love by love and surrounded by love. It's knowing that you are created complete and unbroken, that those around you are created complete and unbroken as well. This knowing is restored to us in The Great Remembering.

Nurturing Our Divine Nature

What's blocking you from embracing love? What ideas or beliefs are determining your frequency and thus creating your reality? Think about the core false beliefs you've identified while working through this book: How have those apparent truths blocked you? What happens when you are presented with messages of the fundamental truth of your wholeness and perfection? How do you respond when you hear that you are perfectly lovable?

If these messages are still difficult to hear, it's a good opportunity to continue the inner work of clearing and nurturing your relationship with your true nature so that you can more fully embrace the love that you are and the love that's available to you. The first step, as always, is awareness. It's noticing how you respond, and then identifying and naming the energy that you're holding about yourself. Embracing love is identifying and naming your core false beliefs, the stories that block your energy and keep you stuck in cycles of addiction, and then moving to a deeper awareness of your true nature, which *is* love.

As we develop this relationship with our divine nature, the love that we are, we become open to something that's always intrinsically been here. This shift can be a process. But it can also happen in an instant. That's what a mystical experience is—those moments when we absolutely know and experience that love is all there is and that we are one with all beings. Embracing love is about expanding our capacity for this experience by cultivating a relationship with our essential selves. This allows us to truly know that love is the ultimate truth of who and what we are.

Another aspect of embracing love is learning to be comfortable with our own company, to be alone and at peace with our ourselves, in every moment. Remember, we are not referring to getting love from the outside, but embracing the love that we are. Osho said it so beautifully when he wrote these powerful words: *"The capacity to be alone is the capacity to love. It may look paradoxical to you, but it's not. It is an existential truth: only those people who are capable of being alone are capable of love, of sharing, of going into the deepest core of another person--without possessing the other, without becoming dependent on the other, without reducing the other to a thing, and without becoming addicted to the other. They allow the other absolute freedom, because they know that if the other leaves, they will be as happy as they are now. Their happiness cannot be taken by the other, because it is not given by the other."*

Inner and Outer Connection

We all have a need to connect with other people; we want to love and receive love. But when we're disconnected from our essential self, our attempts to connect with others are an attempt to feel better, to numb the discomfort of that disconnection. We're trying to use outer love to heal ourselves. But no one person can heal our disconnection; no relationship can bring us to the truth of who and what we are. Nothing "out there" is going to fix what seems broken within. The outer-directed search for connection does not bring the kind of love that heals. It seems contradictory, because we all seem to need to love and connect with others, but that will not return us to a place of inner wholeness. It seems we need both the inner *and* the outer experience of love. It reminds me of the currently popular question: "Why do I keep attracting unavailable people?" My answer to that is simply this: What are you wanting them to be available *for*? Are you wanting a relationship to "fix" you or do your inner work for you? If so, we know this will not work, at least not for long. It is up to each of us to do our own inner work and return to a state of wholeness. Only then do we have something powerful to share with another.

We're often asking the question, "How do I connect with people?" when the deeper question is really, "How do I connect more fully with the essential beingness that I am?" In The Great Remembering, we open to a connection with something that's already there, something we came into this world knowing and *being*. As we come to identify and release the core false beliefs that keep us in cycles of addiction, we're able to *re*-connect, not only with ourselves, but also with other people and the world around us. When we come to understand that we're all one, then there's no more outer and inner, no more "us" and "them," and once we start living this ultimate reality, our lives naturally become full of connection with others. When we live on purpose and embrace the love that is our true self, what we find is that we generally have boundless connections, and boundless energy to nurture those connections. That's the power of The Great Remembering.

To deepen connection, we focus on connection, we practice connection. As connection becomes more familiar to us, our relationship with our divine nature becomes more tangible, our remembering becomes more concrete, which in turn nurtures our external connections. It all needs our attention. Where we put our focus matters, just as how we direct our behavior matters. We can focus our attention through tools and practices for deepening connection, like those covered in part 2, including building safe community, meditation, living in the question, and so on. These tools and practices can help us deepen connection. Community, for one, presents us with a rich truth: The more we connect with others in a safe community, the more connected we are with ourselves; and the more connected we are with ourselves, the more connected we can be with others.

Cultivating Supportive Community

When we're around like-minded and like-hearted people, it magnifies whatever it is that we share. This can seem positive or negative. If we're hanging around people who share our sense of shame or who share our belief that the world is dangerous, then those "realities" only become stronger. So, looking at your community can be as simple as asking, "Are my friends supporting a larger vision for my life? Or, are they contributing to my sense of feeling stuck?" As you grow in connection with your true self and with ultimate reality, you may find that the friends who are not supportive of your spiritual growth will start to drift away, and you begin gravitating toward and attracting people who lift you up, people who are on the same path, people who can reflect the truth of who and what you are during those times when you forget.

As the power of a supportive community begins to shift things in your life, you may even sometimes experience what looks like chaos. Nurturing community can be a wonderful opportunity to see other levels of spiritual growth that are possible. This can create the experience of "chemicalization;" that crumbling of the material world that I described in the preface. It occurs when our consciousness is shifting in a positive way and the external world starts to fall apart because it does not support our new level of awareness, or it was built on shaky ground. This can, at first, appear to be a "terrible" thing, if we aren't conscious of how we are viewing it and speaking about it.

Those are the moments when it's important to recognize that

what we call it matters. Our language has power. We can call it a terrible thing, we can call it conflict, we can call it a change, we can call it a moment of transition. Or we can think in quantum terms and call it a shift in energy that signals to us that something else is emerging. We can choose to open our perspective to its fullest and accept whatever is there. It means that in the midst of whatever's happening, we can be grateful for the amazing thing that's going to evolve out of it. What a spectacular gift. Asking the question: "What wants to be born here?" can assist us in these times of uncertainty.

Another great gift of connection is that it opens us up to experiencing more joy in our lives. When we are more connected to our essential self, to our divine nature, then our connections with others don't bear all the weight that they once did. Our connections with others are no longer responsible for our healing or our recovery; we're no longer connecting with others *in order to* feel better about ourselves. We're connecting with others out of a place of oneness with our ultimate self. From that place our intention is to share love, rather than to make love happen or to experience love. "Being loved" doesn't matter so much anymore because we literally live *in* love and *as* love.

And the thing is, as we share love from this deeper place, we do end up "getting" more love. Again, that's the power of connection from a place of fundamental wholeness. It's the difference between being *loved* and being *love*. There is a paradox here, as there often is. We also recognize the profound impact that unconditional love has on the people around us. Can you remember a person in your life that absolutely loved you unconditionally? Do you remember the profoundly positive effect this had on your life? This is a simple reminder that the more we do the work of inner clearing and live in the world *as* love, the more positive impact we have on the people around us and the world at large.

Perceiving Reality

A spiritual journey is not about eradicating perceived difficult life situations. It's not about avoiding or denying problems or challenges. As we grow in awareness, we recognize that apparent problems or challenges can be approached from endless perspectives. How we see what is happening is a choice, and what we call the events in relative reality goes a long way to creating that reality. Coming from a place of wholeness, of integration, we are more likely to choose to focus on transformation, creativity, connection, and love. This speaks to the proverbial question: Is the glass half empty or half full? My response is this: The master knows it is both half empty and half full. In that way, the master is free to choose how to view life, without needing to deny anything or feel a need to change anyone else's point of view. We can see endless possibilities in every situation.

How we perceive reality creates how we experience reality. Your awareness of this truth, no matter how you come to it, combined with a deep relationship with your essential self, is what brings peace and happiness. A shift in perspective can open us to infinite possibilities. As Milton wrote over three hundred years ago, *"The mind is its own place, and in itself it can make a Heav'n of Hell, a Hell of Heav'n."* From there, all the strategies, stories, and beliefs that have kept us limited look and feel different. They don't look like the ultimate truth anymore. Instead they look small and insignificant and so it's easier to release them. That's divine integration, and it's where everything begins to happen. This doesn't mean *only* flipping things into a positive story. We can't trick the universe. Sure, when we experience this integration, what we call "reality" tends to become more open and we experience more love and connection and see more potential. But it won't work to try to bypass the inner work that makes this possible.

Spiritual Bypassing

Sometimes we try to avoid or sidetrack dealing with the difficult aspects of human life by using spiritual concepts and practices to "spiritually bypass" the things we do not want to face. We *pretend* that we do not feel angry, resentful, or hurt by somebody else's words or actions. We believe that it is "not spiritual" to feel these emotions. Possibly, on a subconscious level, we would rather not deal with them, or we are afraid to look. Perhaps from another level of consciousness we would not have the same emotional reactions; however, it is important to be honest with ourselves about where we are. Allowing ourselves to compassionately practice present-moment awareness is a tool we can use for walking *through* these experiences rather than bypassing them.

I tried to make such a spiritual bypass for quite some time. I believed I could "bypass" the more deeply rooted core beliefs I was holding about myself and the world. I started *pretending* to be "oh so spiritual" which to me, at that level of conscious awareness, meant not acknowledging any of the challenges I was experiencing. That was how I saw it from my perspective at the time. I was living from a spiritual level that I call "magical thinking." This wasn't incorrect. It was just where I was at during that stage of my evolution. When I did break through to a deeper level of awareness and surrender to a source of inner strength, I started to experience a dynamic power that naturally emerged. I had tapped into a Source that's stronger than any external force imaginable. It was then that my outer life suddenly started matching that powerful frequency. The nuance here is that it's not about "acting as if." It's not about *getting* the outer world to align with our inner connectedness so that we can prove how enlightened we are. That approach is still grounded in resistance and judgment.

Things don't truly change until we allow ourselves to become fully integrated, which to me, means the union of what we might call "spiritual" with what we might call "human." As we've seen throughout this book, it's the inner work that uncovers our core false beliefs, and it's the practicing of spiritual principles that allows us to unlearn habits of judgment and resistance. It's the inner work that lets us release the stories created by experiences of trauma and shame. It's the inner work that breaks the cycle of addiction we've created to protect ourselves from a world we believe is unloving and dangerous. It's the inner work that brings us to a U-turn in consciousness, to an awareness that our beliefs are relative, not ultimate reality.

Divine Integration

When we expand our perspective, when we loosen our hold on "the truth," we allow ourselves to see what else is there. We integrate the "positive" and the "negative." The pessimist comes to see that there is not only pain, but also joy and transformation. The optimist learns to open to feelings of sadness and loss, to make peace with impermanence. Wherever you are coming from, whatever your core false beliefs, spiritual integration means honoring and integrating all aspects of ourselves so that we can see things in a fuller, more authentic light. When we shift our awareness, our inner sense, to the ultimate reality of who and what we are, we experience a level of consciousness from which we see all experience as spiritual experience.

At this level, we welcome all of life—health and disease, marriage and divorce, sadness and joy. This spiritual consciousness rejects nothing, accepts everything. It embraces what's in the shadow. In fact, welcoming it all might be the highest degree of spiritual integration, letting us live in and through the transformative power of even the most painful situations. It's being present to what is. And then, paradoxically, when we master this, life seems to give us more and more to be joyful about. Our pain lessens and we experience more love, connection, and happiness.

The more time you spend in silence, the more comfortable you become in your spiritual practices, the more you will enjoy a loving relationship with your essential self. The more you know that self and the more you integrate that deep knowing, the more you can *be* love in the world. Whenever we can be free from clinging and averting, free from judging, we tap into pure awareness. There are several stories of people throughout the history of humankind who have lived in a continuous state of mystical awareness. And times are changing, which is opening the possibility for more and more of us to awaken to this greater way of *being*. What was once for a few; Lao Tzu, Buddha, Jesus, for example, is now a possibility for us all. We are entering into a new era of conscious evolution where this deeper awareness is not only possible, but happening within more of us every day.

Whenever we absolutely know and feel the truth of who we are, when we know that we are love, then we can live *as* love in the world, in the midst of whatever is happening. That's integration. If we know we *are* love, then we're able to show up *as* love. We're able to live in questions like, "How would love show up *here*? What would love do *here*? Where would love be present *here*?" And here, in the midst of it all, is where love is needed the most.

Chapter Nine

AWAKENED LIVING

It is the birthright of each and every one of us to live an awakened life. Most religions and spiritual traditions teach us that we need to adopt a certain belief system or follow some prescribed steps in order to attain a state of enlightenment. A long-held belief about awakening is that only a small number of people, destined to become gurus or spiritual teachers, can attain it. It is certainly true that until recent times only a small minority of people on the planet had attained this state of full self-realization. These saints, mystics, and spiritual masters were seen as "special." And they certainly were, at the time. However, times are changing. We are now living in an era of rapid acceleration of the phenomenon of spiritual awakening. The truth is that awakening is absolutely available to every single human being on the planet right here, right now. Enlightenment is our most natural state. When we strip away all the concepts and ideas we have learned over our lifetime— about ourselves and how we view the world—we uncover the simple truth.

— *TJ Woodward, Conscious Being*

Living an awakened life is fundamentally simple. It's our natural state. Awakened living is waking up from the illusion of separation, fear, and scarcity, and returning to our original perfection. Awakened living is experiencing absolute presence, and living in a state of awe and wonder. It's living beyond our stories of shame and trauma, and living in a state of curiosity that's possible because we are grounded in love and community in an ever-growing relationship with our essential self. Awakened Living is a recognition that the basis of our life is freedom and the purpose of our life is joy.

As we've seen throughout this book, we nurture this relationship and live an awakened life through spiritual practices such as mindfulness exercises and building safe spiritual community. We grow in awareness by identifying our core false beliefs, questioning the assumptions we make in our ego state, and practicing nonjudgment and nonresistance to come more fully aligned with our authentic self. When we truly recognize our oneness with Spirit, we're living beyond judgment. We're living in radical forgiveness, love and joy. Life is no longer something that happens *to* us. It's something that happens not only *through* us, but *as* us. We *are* love, we *are* forgiveness, we *are* joy!

Finding Purpose

When we talk about purpose, we generally refer to something in the outer realm, something we want to *do*. We tend to believe that if we achieve this thing or that thing, then we will acquire what we want, whether that's fulfillment or happiness or a better standard of living. We often look at our goals and achievements as effort, striving, even as struggle. What we're discovering together in this book is the power of the inward-looking approach. Tapping into our wholeness, into our divine nature, is our most fundamental purpose. Our primary purpose is simply to awaken. Being grounded in that space of essential wholeness makes pursuing any intention in the outer realm much easier, more powerful and connected. When we tap into the truth of who and what we are, life naturally becomes purposeful. There's no striving to achieve something beyond us. We are simply guided in a very powerful way to what's already there.

I want to examine two levels of purpose: our common inner purpose and our individual, outer-directed purposes. Our fundamental purpose is simply to awaken—to become conscious of our inherent wholeness, to live in a state of presence, to become aware of our oneness with Source. And as we grow in awareness of this purpose, it becomes manifest in all our outer-directed purposes. This isn't about figuring it out. It isn't about latching onto a new set of beliefs or perfecting our spiritual technique to do it correctly. It's about deepening the awareness of our essential wholeness. It's also about moving from our head, into our heart, and ultimately living in a deep awareness of our intuition. It is shifting from feeling trapped by our thoughts and ego-driven goals into experiencing a deeper, more authentic feeling tone. It is expressing a fundamentally new way of being in the world. This is the most profound journey, because as we move into this intuition-based, inner-directed way of living, everything changes.

This deep vision of the self is the fruit of your spiritual practice, your inner work. It comes from your essential being. It is beyond thought and beyond emotion. This deeper vision is your most important purpose; it's what you may have been experiencing throughout your recovery and throughout the pages of this book. As you move more deeply into recognizing your oneness with Source, you will also be opened to a vision specific to your individual life. As you live more fully in connection and love, you'll glimpse a distinct purpose that's tied to the universal purpose, which is to remember and live from our essential wholeness and perfection. The deep trust of your inner knowing will guide and inform you about your own way of serving humanity and the world.

Ego and Purpose

As I shared previously, when I had been in recovery for a time, I had accomplished a great deal of success in the outer realm. I had a prosperous business, a handsome boyfriend, and a muscular body. I had been practicing spiritual principles like affirmations and mediation, and I was finding safety in spiritual community. I was taking ownership of my thoughts and intentions. My life seemed complete. Yet, in the midst of all this external success and inner growth, I started experiencing a vision of myself as a spiritual teacher. My inner voice began revealing to me that my purpose was to deepen my own awakening. And my purpose was also to bring this transformation into the world. I couldn't see how that vision was possible, so whenever I felt it, my ego mind would say, "That's crazy. You can't do that! How could that happen? How could you make a living from that?" Even as my ego mind tried to dampen the vision, it quietly persisted, all the time getting stronger and more clear. Back and forth I went, between the vision and my doubt, as I stayed open both to what my deepest self was offering and to my desire to control the situation.

When at last I finally said yes to that vision, my outer world began to crumple. I went through a time of personal chaos as my current life met with this new consciousness. Things needed to break and expand, so I could accept the vision, because it was so much bigger than what my current perspective and my existing way of life could handle. Because my ego was so quickly shutting down my visions, they required nurturing. Once I said yes to my personal vision, I consciously and intentionally began moving that yes into a deeper, more profound awareness. In this ongoing process, I came to embrace the feeling tone of my authentic personal purpose.

When this kind of nurturing doesn't happen, or when we ignore our visions entirely, they can easily disappear. During a workshop a few years ago, one of the participants came to see that her own vision for life was something to do with helping animals. At the moment this happened, we could see it come to life in her physically. It looked like twenty years fell away instantly; she suddenly had this lightness about her. However, almost immediately, her ego mind crept in and she started saying things like, "What about my job?" and "I can't go to veterinary school at my age!" Just as suddenly, we saw that expansiveness close back down. The light was soon dimmed.

You may have experienced this yourself: first feeling the joy of that peak spiritual experience in which you're in touch with a vision, and then letting the ego tear it away from you with "I can't" and "that won't work." Visions are delicate; think of them as an energy that needs honing, a frequency that needs fine-tuning through attention to our spiritual practice and our community. Once we get our vision, it is necessary to create a space in which it can thrive and manifest. That might mean surrounding ourselves with people who want to support it. It might mean not sharing the vision with anyone for a while as we sit with it in meditation, allowing the silence to bring it more fully to our conscious awareness. It's like a tiny sprout that needs fertilizing and tending indoors before it's strong enough to withstand the elements.

Maintaining Focus

Nurturing your revelation is about eradicating everything in your life and in your consciousness that dampens your vision. Think of this old story about a frog race. One day, a bunch of pond frogs decided to race to the top of a nearby tree. As a group, they headed for the tree, while all the frogs who stayed behind muttered to each other: "This ought to be good. They'll never make it." As the frogs started up the lower part of the tree, the crowd started shouting: "You're kidding yourselves!" "It's too tall!" Some of the frogs soon dropped from the tree, but others kept going. The crowd kept shouting, "You'll die if you go any farther!" and more frogs fell. Eventually there was only one frog left, and he was undeterred—finally managing to reach the top of the tree. When he had made his way back to the pond they all asked, "How did you do it?" He didn't answer. They raised their voices and shouted at him, "What's your secret, friend?" Still no answer. Finally, an old frog who had been watching the entire time said quietly, "Why are you shouting at him? He's deaf."

Once you get a hold of a vision for your life and decide it's what you truly desire, be like that frog, carefully immune to all the voices of doom that tell you it isn't possible. How much could you accomplish if you were free from those voices in your life? When you do listen to those voices, they can sometimes even activate your old core false beliefs. This might happen even when you're living in conscious awareness. So, I want to encourage you to return always to the practice and process of unlearning. We continuously need to unlearn, no matter our level of conscious awareness. We constantly need to nurture our purpose and our intention. Sometimes this takes time. I once held a vision for my life for about two years before it started manifesting in the outer realm. Once it did, things moved more rapidly and doors commenced to open. But those were two long years, and if I had not been nurturing my vision through spiritual discipline, I could easily have given up.

I nurture my purpose in relative reality as well as ultimate reality. On the inner level, I utilize meditation, for example, to remain in touch with my foundational wholeness and to nurture the relationship with my divine nature. I also foster my purpose on the level of relative reality—in the outer world of practicality and actionable goals. For example, I make it a point to set concrete and measurable goals for myself. I am blessed with three people who have committed to supporting my purpose. I am accountable to them. We meet every Monday to go over my current intention and my current action items. Every week I report to all three of them: Here's what I did do, and here's what I didn't do. This is the sort of tangible, practical support that helps me nurture my outer purpose.

Conscious Action

Action is still required. In an awakened life, it's very different than the outer-driven action we may be accustom to living. There's more ease and more grace. It's not about achieving something in order to be successful or to be accepted or acceptable; it's about doing something that's nourishing us internally, something that comes out of who and what we essentially are. So, we can live in gratitude for every single action item; every task is now an expression of our vision. It's a truly different way of being in the world. Don't worry if you haven't discovered your personal life vision. Growing in awareness of who and what you are is your fundamental purpose. The more you live in *that* purpose, the more apparent your own individual outer purpose will become. And, as you align more closely with your purpose, the people and the tools to support your vision will flow more easily into your life. The world will help guide you into what's next.

A word about ego: In many spiritual practices and traditions, it is taught that the goal is to be rid of the ego. As my wonderful friend and colleague Dr. Sue Morter so eloquently stated: *"Only ego would want ego to die."* So, rather than viewing your ego as something to be destroyed, I invite you to open up to a new way of seeing it. In the awakened state, the ego becomes the vehicle for Spirit. In other words, the ego holds within it aspects of personality that can be useful in your life and in this world when married with a powerful vision and intention. In my own life, I am grateful that I have certain talents that allow me to deliver my message of spiritual awakening to a large audience. What are the gifts of your ego?

Choosing Happiness

Our culture tells us that happiness is something to be achieved. Often we act as if our purpose in life is to find happiness, whether it be through achieving what looks like success or freeing ourselves from pain. The trouble with anything we "get" in that way is that we then may believe we need to hang onto it, to fight for it, or we might fear we will lose it. The Dalai Lama says this about happiness: *"When you are discontent, you always want more, more, more. Your desire can never be satisfied. But when you practice contentment, you can say to yourself, 'Oh yes - I already have everything that I really need.'"* We might look at happiness as something granted to the lucky few. Our stories, our core beliefs, might tell us that happiness is beyond us, that it's only for other people. But if we believe that happiness is just the luck of the draw, as it were, if it's available to some and out of reach for others, that's a roadmap to despair. Fortunately, we can experience happiness in a different way as we awaken to our true self. We begin to experience happiness as a choice.

For some, this can be hard to imagine or accept. In fact, out of all the discussions I have with people about spiritual awakening, this is the one that results in the most push-back and resistance. "Happiness is a choice? I'm not sure if I can buy that." "Really? Do you know what you're saying to people who have depression or are suffering from a debilitating illness?" So, first let me clarify what I mean by happiness. Happiness in this sense is more than a feeling. It's more than a rush of ecstasy, more than having a great day or even a great year, more than the experience of health or the absence of pain. It's more than the security that comes with external success. Further, happiness is not simply flipping the story, or looking for the good in all things. It's a state of contentment, and a level of satisfaction with *what is*. We might call it *joy*.

In the book *How We Choose to Be Happy* by Greg Hicks and R. F. Foster, the authors interviewed people from around the world—both happy people and unhappy people. They found nine basic choices that truly happy people have made. These are not attributes, activities, or feelings. They're choices. You might be surprised to hear that one of the choices happy people make is the choice to feel emotions deeply. Happy people choose to embrace *all* their feelings. When happy people lose someone, they hurt, they grieve, they feel loss. Loss and sorrow are just as much a part of an authentic, integrated life as feelings of satisfaction and joy. When truly happy people allow themselves to feel deeply, those feelings pass through them, which allows them to return to their natural state of presence and joy.

Choosing Peace

How can you make this kind of choice? How can you choose peace and happiness in every moment, regardless of outer circumstances? It's all about awareness. If you're trapped by your unconscious biases and assumptions, then those things are running the show and making your choices *for you*. Those mental structures are unconsciously dictating what you feel, and what you push into the shadow. From that level of awareness, you can't *seem* to choose happiness. You can't seem to choose because you don't know you can. But as you begin to identify those limiting inner constructs, those deeply held beliefs about yourself and the world, then more possibilities become open to you. As your awareness deepens, so does your experience of freedom, including the freedom to choose peace and happiness. And this comes from a state of consciousness, a way of being in the world. Yes, peace and happiness are both states of being in the world. They are choices.

Happiness and peace are decisions we make. We can decide that no matter what happens, we're going to be open-hearted, loving, and connected. Even when we lose touch with that choice and seem to get bumped off track, as when something happens to trigger our fight, flight, or freeze responses, we can still return to this choice. Peace is what makes this happiness choice possible. Peace is the sense that we don't need anything or anyone to change in order to experience a deep sense of contentment and joy. It's the assurance that our freedom is not limited by how things are in the external world.

One might imagine that living in a state of peace and happiness puts us in a state of denial about all the seeming pain and injustice in the world. But choosing peace and happiness doesn't require us to look the other way when we're confronted by its *seeming* opposite. In fact, it's the confidence of peace and the power of happiness that allows us to infuse every situation with love and forgiveness. It's what makes peaceful resistance so effective, it's what energizes the lives of people like Mahatma Gandhi and Martin Luther King, Jr. When we are grounded in oneness with Source we can approach even the most violent situation without succumbing to the reactive impulse. And when we're free from the impulse to fight back, to fix things, to beat up the "bad guy," our vision expands and we can experience other possibilities. This is what it means to live an awakened life.

Discovering True Freedom

Our culture is all about freedom. People often speak of fighting for freedom or protecting freedom from the enemy. We tend to think about freedom as something to be gained or lost on the outside—something granted to us by external things, like our constitution, government, or lifestyle. And we fear it can be taken from us by external things, like our nation's enemies, the penal system, our boss, or our addiction. I'd like to look at a different type of freedom—one that is not freedom from anything external. Simply put, this is an inner freedom from duality, from "good" "bad" "right" and "wrong." It's freedom from the stories and perspectives that limit our choices and viewpoints. This freedom opens us to the power of authenticity, to the choice of peace and happiness, to awakened living.

This doesn't mean that in a state of freedom we are not ever going to notice we have opinions or perspectives; it simply means that we are not as deeply entrenched or invested in our opinions and perspectives. We recognize their place in the spectrum of possible options. We see our opinions and perspectives as an expression of who we are and what we are experiencing *at this moment,* given what we know and what we don't know. Our opinions and perspectives are not the totality of who and what we are. Furthermore, as we continue on our path of awakening, we *can* actually raise our consciousness and move beyond opinions and perspectives altogether. Freedom is then possible and we arrive at a place of witnessing life rather than reacting to it. It's being in a state of awareness of nonresistance and non-judgment that allows us to evaluate our opinions and perspectives and choose from there. Are our opinions causing conflict and division? If they are, our freedom opens us up to the other sides of the story, to possible alternatives. Is our perspective bringing something valuable to a relationship or situation? If it is, our freedom opens us up to adding further to that perspective, to nurturing it with additional information and deeper nuance.

Inner freedom is living in present moment awareness. It is a level of consciousness that's beyond clinging and aversion, beyond suffering. That to me is what is meant by *"Being in the world but not of it."* When we're of this world, we are bounced around by life, reacting to what happens *to* us, imprisoned by the stories we've built up about ourselves and our world. When we're in this world but *not* of it, we still move through relative reality, but we're grounded in our absolute essence, and this provides unlimited freedom to choose, to feel fully without being manipulated, and to respond rather than react to the fluctuations of the outer world.

Moving toward freedom may seem like a process, and not a one-time event. Things in the outer realm can sometimes pull us back toward old behaviors when we are early in our spiritual practice. Just because we are growing in awareness doesn't mean that daily "challenges" will suddenly stop appearing. Our spiritual practices keep us aware, helping us to return consistently and constantly, moment to moment, back to a state of love and connection. Freedom may take practice, and as things like meditation and mindfulness teach us to become more aware of our reactive self, we become able to witness the reactive self without judgment and then to question it. We can ask what choices we have to make in the situation. There are always deeper levels to freedom; indeed, becoming patient with this process is a kind of freedom in itself. Are you ready to release and let go of the self-imposed prison you have been living within? This is the moment!

Embodying the New Paradigm

Michael Bernard Beckwith so eloquently stated: *"We're not here to save the world, we're here to serve the new paradigm."* Spiritual teachers have long taught us that we are more than human beings who now and again have a spiritual experience; we are spiritual beings having a human experience. This has been an important insight for humanity. But it's often still grounded in binary thinking, in a duality between physical and spiritual. Today humanity is entering another level of consciousness—the emerging recognition that we are spiritual beings having a spiritual experience. This awareness of the underlying unity of all allows us to welcome things we might otherwise see as "negative," like disease, unemployment, and death, as well as the experiences we've tended to see as "positive," like a new baby, a promotion, or falling in love. It's all part of the rich tapestry of an authentic and awakened life.

When we live from this mystical awareness, we live with a feeling tone that everything is spiritual (meaning we recognize the greater reality of oneness beneath all situations), and we no longer attempt to cling to the "positive" or eradicate the "negative." We no longer avoid either light or shadow. From this space of consciousness, we can be the observer. We can recognize that everything is fuel for transformation, and yes, some of the most painful experiences can be the most transformative. So, even as we enter into something painful, even as we're feeling that pain deeply, the spiritual perspective allows us to ask, "What is wanting to be born here?" This openness to Spirit in all things is the new paradigm. It's a space beyond duality, a space of stillness in the essential self. This new paradigm is beyond any one perspective, beyond any single story, fully grounded in present moment awareness, in curiosity, awe, and wonder. What's more, the new paradigm takes much less effort than the old. Duality is hard work. If we're stuck seeing the world through the lens of "us" and "them," then compassion can be difficult, gratitude and generosity challenging, and forgiveness may seem almost impossible.

When we awaken to the deeper understanding that we're all

one, we experience an immense shift. In this paradigm, we may sometimes still experience pain, but we will no longer blame anyone or any situation as the *cause* of the pain. We will be accountable for our own experience. It may be that a wound within us is touched by what happened, and in that case, it's important to discover how it might help us grow beyond that trigger. As a matter of fact, we no longer focus on triggers at all, but acknowledge that something is activated within us that is wanting to heal. In that way, we can welcome every situation as an opportunity for our own growth and expansion. When we come to see that what other people do or say doesn't impact the truth of who and what we are, and we recognize they are acting out of their own "woundology," we don't make ourselves victims to anyone else's behavior. We no longer blame anyone else for our experiences. We become able to respond to them rather than reacting out of our old programming. In this way, we can be at peace regardless of outer circumstances.

As we embody this dynamic new paradigm, new possibilities open in our consciousness and in our lives. We recognize that because we have grown in conscious awareness, we can naturally access and activate a deeper blueprint for our lives. We can embrace a life filled with connection and joy. We find ourselves living from a perspective of continuous awe and wonder. Life becomes immensely simpler over time, and we move into a way of being that even feels *effortless*. This is because we have awakened into a new way of seeing ourselves and the world. We have been returned to our original perfection. Because of this, our lives continue to open to greater opportunities. As we grow our level of consciousness, the outer world responds.

Awakening into Service

When we tap into a deeper vision for life, it can literally bring us to life, because the visions that come from our oneness with Source call us to be more fully authentic. Interestingly, in most cases, those visions involve serving other people. It has been said that a truly fulfilling life includes serving others in some way. That has certainly been my experience. People who are living authentically in love and connection often do not envision *just* living in order to get more stuff or more power, it quite often also includes helping humanity in some way. There's something about living in true freedom that leads us toward serving as a catalyst for contributing to the world. Mahatma Gandhi said it this way: *"Service which is rendered without joy helps neither the servant nor the served. But all other pleasures issued possessions pale into nothingness before service which is rendered in a spirit of joy."*

The greatest form of service we can offer the world is nurturing and growing into a state of present awareness, living *as* love and connection. When we're living in a state of conscious awareness, our very being helps shift the greater consciousness on the planet. So, the first and best way to be of service is to do our own inner work of clearing. From that consciousness of freedom, each of us chooses how we serve the world. We often think of "service to others" as something that is offered from a place of superiority. We see it as sacrifice, as giving up something. Per a dualistic paradigm, if we are "good people" we will give from the store of what we have to those who have less. This assumes many things. It might assume that service involves someone who has more, knows more, or is worth more. It might mean giving up something to a person who has less, knows less, or is worth less. So right from the start, this service is based on duality, and it both assumes and encourages an unequal relationship. Our service can be all tangled up with a martyr/victim consciousness.

Let's say you decide to get involved in helping the homeless. If you approach this undertaking as a sacrifice of what you possess, then you may end up creating more suffering. This approach tends to put you, the "giver," in a position that's superior to that of the "receiver." This relationship may set up certain expectations that limit understanding and diminish your service. For instance, it may lead you to make assumptions about what the person in front of you needs, without knowing anything more about them. You may be more tempted to judge them and to resist information that challenges your judgment. Or you may be crippled by guilt that you have plenty while they do not.

But if you come to service from a space of present moment awareness, from a space of oneness, you will be free from judgment and resistance, able to remain more present, more authentic, more open to what people are saying, and more relaxed about your work. When you are open, you allow others to open, and this is a large part of any service. This makes the service that we're called to in an awakened life so much more graceful and rich than what we might have experienced before. Our awareness shapes our service. Our every moment, our every act, is formed by our consciousness, our way of being in the world. So, that most fundamental and universal human service—growing in awareness and living an awakened life—leads each of us into our own unique forms of service—whether that be working with the homeless, helping to preserve wildlife habitat, serving as a mentor or coach, or even discovering that we have a powerful and innovative way of serving humanity as a whole. Whatever we do, living in a state of open awareness will lead to and shape authentic service. It starts in consciousness and it ends in consciousness.

Engaging an Enlightened Life

Enlightenment is an inside job. Nothing on the outside needs to change for you to be happy, free, and living the most awakened version of your life. As you recognize how the beliefs, stories, and perspectives that initially protected you may now be limiting your freedom and your choice, you can move into the process of living in oneness with Source. As you wake up, you have more freedom and more choice. This is both a process and a moment-by-moment decision to remember the truth of who and what you are. You can live in a state of awe, wonder and peace, and you can choose happiness.

In *being* peace and happiness, in demonstrating it to yourself and to others, you serve the world. Bringing the new paradigm to life is the ultimate service, and the greatest gift you can offer. Humans are designed to grow. As we reach one level of understanding, we tend to yearn for a deeper awareness. When we come up against the limits of our current state, our current beliefs or strategies, we may experience discomfort or imbalance. When we're able to be with that discomfort, we can see where it comes from and where it's headed. And so we grow. Wherever we are, whatever our level of consciousness, we can grow, we can become more fully aware, more fully awakened.

Enlightenment is actually a very ordinary state. It is also an extra-ordinary state. It feels elevated because it is not burdened by all the weighty ideas and beliefs we had previously amassed. When we come to realize the truth of who and what we are, we are no longer limited by the false sense of identity within which we had previously been confined. Our natural state of freedom is restored. There is no longer anything to fear. The deep peace of our true nature is revealed to us. We are no longer run by the programs in our mind—that is, our learned ideas about who we are and how we "should" live, including our concepts of "right and wrong," and "good and bad." We have remembered that we are pure consciousness. Consciousness simply is. It is not for or against anything. It simply *is* everything. When we are fully self-realized, we naturally speak and act *as* love. We could not possibly do or be anything else.

In Conclusion

Let's look at how far you've come. Think back to the moment (or moments) when you first realized that your addictive behavior was no longer serving you. When you first acknowledged that your search in the outer realm wasn't going to fix things—no amount of alcohol, work, sex, shopping, or any other addictive behavior could restore you to a place of wholeness. You came to believe that somehow an awareness of love and connection was possible for you, even though you couldn't see it or even imagine it. That step took courage. It took trust in your recovery.

Now, think back to when you were first recognizing and releasing your core false beliefs. Remember that painful "aha" moment when you realized that on deep level you truly did believe you were unlovable, or unworthy, or whatever? When you truly felt how deeply uncomfortable that false narrative was because it wasn't your true self? When you saw that the reality you had created from your core false beliefs was not the reality you desired? That step took a willingness to reach down into the shadow and welcome it up to the surface. That step took conviction. It took trust in the process.

Remember that moment when you first wondered if maybe another way was possible? And remember when you started realizing that you are not your beliefs, your stories, your old narratives, your reactions? Remember when you were able to take that next step into the unknown, into a new relationship with yourself and with Source? Remember the joy and excitement you experienced when you remembered a deeper truth of who and what you truly are? That step took imagination. It took trust in yourself.

Recovery means a restoration to health. It is a restoration to your essential self. It is a restoration of the beautiful infinite potential you were born with, free from all the limited and limiting distortions of those old stories and false beliefs, and full of possibility, curiosity, and awe. That restoration is your divine vision, your ultimate purpose as a human. *Conscious Recovery* restores you to this place. It returns you to this perfectly recovered canvas. And once you're there, you can consciously create whatever portrait your oneness with Source reveals to you. And you can *be* that self, that vision, much more deeply than when you identified with your old misrepresentations of limitation and brokenness.

You have the power to open your heart to a new way of being. You have the power to experience a deep sense of gratitude, peace, and happiness. This power is within you, right here and right now. All you need to do is say yes. Are you ready?

A gentle reminder of the truth:

You are Whole

You are Perfect

You are Magnificent

You deserve a life filled with love, connection and joy.

You have the power to consciously create the life of your dreams.

THE MOMENT IS NOW!

For more in-depth exploration of my Conscious Recovery process, please sign up for my FREE 7-day video e-course:

www.TJWoodwardFreeGift.com

Made in the USA
Columbia, SC
01 September 2019